BENJAMIN CASON RAWLINGS

First Virginia Volunteer for the South

Benjamin Cason Rawlings

This image of Benjamin C. Rawlings was taken in Petersburg. At that time, the uniformed Rawlings was a seventeen-year-old lieutenant.

From the author's collection.

BENJAMIN CASON RAWLINGS

First Virginia Volunteer for the South

by

Byrd Barnette Tribble

1st Edition
Butternut and Blue
1995

ISBN 0-935523-47-2

Published in 1996
as the fifth volume of
the *Army of Northern Virginia Series*

BUTTERNUT AND BLUE
3411 Northwind Road
Baltimore, Maryland 21234
410-256-9220

For Jim

CONTENTS

* * * * * * * * * * *

MAPS AND ILLUSTRATIONS

* * * * * * * * * * *

INTRODUCTION

In the summer of 1904, Benjamin Cason Rawlings sat down on the front porch of his home near Raphine, Virginia, and began to dictate his Civil War Reminiscences to his son, James Emery Rawlings. The old Confederate soldier suffered from heart disease and found the task of writing down his experiences a taxing one. A few years earlier, he had written a narrative of his unpleasant life as a Union prisoner of war, but the most compelling part of his story remained to be told. Indeed, his story is one of a young Virginian engaged in a quest of heroic proportions, punctuated at times by comedy and reckless adventure.

The bare facts of his actions are a litany of deeds admired by an approving Southern society: In December, 1860, when he was fifteen years old, Rawlings set out from his home in Spotsylvania County, Virginia, without telling his parents, journeyed to Charleston, and enlisted in Company A of the First South Carolina Volunteers. His regiment was engaged during the bombardment of Fort Sumter and later in April, 1861, enjoyed a triumphal welcome in Richmond as the first troops to come to Virginia from another Confederate state. He then joined the Thirtieth Virginia Infantry Regiment and was with that unit at Antietam, September 17, 1862, when the Thirtieth Virginia suffered heavy casualties in action near the Dunkard Church. He was captured during Mine Run Campaign of November, 1863, "starved at Point Lookout," and was exchanged in October, 1864. During the final months of the war, he defended the Petersburg lines with his regiment, which, as part of Corse's Brigade of Pickett's Division, fought at Dinwiddie Courthouse, Sayler's Creek, and "stood fast to the end at Five Forks." Rawlings was part of the remnant of Pickett's command to reach Appomattox.

Because he had gone to Charleston and had enlisted in the South Carolina regiment, Rawlings was celebrated as a Southern hero even before the Civil War began. In the winter of 1861, Virginia and South Carolina newspapers reported his presence in Charleston as a Virginia volunteer for the South. Family letters demonstrate the pride which his relatives felt in his accomplishments; his South Carolina colonel admired his "high spirit;" a prominent South Carolinian considered him one "of the true grit." Back home in Virginia, he was the local hero who had seen the white flag at Fort Sumter. In going to Charleston, he acted out what many other Southern youths aspired to do but had not dared. Ben Rawlings' mystique as a veteran of Fort Sumter set him above and apart from his fellow soldiers in the Thirtieth Virginia. The troops of that regiment expected him to be a brave, courageous soldier and a leader of men. Evidently they were not disappointed because they elected Ben Rawlings first lieutenant of Company D in 1862, when he was seventeen years old.

Ben Rawlings' *Reminiscences* are personal, impressionistic, and anecdotal -- not military or political history but autobiography, the story of the most culturally significant segment of his life. As Ben Rawlings the narrator in 1904 selected the experiences that he would dictate, he often chose anecdotes instead of detailed descriptions of battles. He seemed to view Ben Rawlings, the youthful protagonist, with benevolence and amusement as he recalled the often-comic drama played out by his younger persona. He related in detail his experiences as an artless, sixteen-year-old private whose messmates gulled him into believing that he had to fight a duel with a South Carolina lieutenant to defend the honor of his beloved Virginia. Although many of his stories are comic, he included several incidents which reveal both a genuine respect for his own youthful accomplishments and an awareness of the pathos of war. He was obviously proud of his promotion to captain at the age of eighteen while "under fire and in line of battle" during the siege of Suffolk in 1863. When Rawlings described the grim reality of war, he exhibited a keen sense of irony in such stories as that of the lieutenant, who before the Battle of Antietam, remarked to Rawlings that they were both dangerously conspicuous in their red hunting shirts. Later Rawlings tells us that he found his friend in the red shirt "lying at the foot of a tree near the Dunkard Church with a daguerreotype of his sweetheart in his hand and shot through the breast dead."

The Virginia society whose ideals Ben Rawlings reflected was one in which an individual belonged to his family in a profound and vital sense. It was a society seriously concerned with family credentials and worthy ancestors. The Rawlings family came to

Maryland from England in the seventeenth century. By 1728, one of their number, a James Rawlings, had moved from Maryland to Spotsylvania County to expand the family iron mining and processing business. He bought land along the north bank of the Pamunkey River (later called the North Anna), where he mined and farmed. Patriotic ancestors included at least two men who served as soldiers in the American Revolution. In 1860, several branches of the Rawlings family lived comfortably on plantations of moderate size in Spotsylvania and Orange counties. Most were Baptists but a few retained the old family allegiance to the Episcopal Church, formerly, of course, the Church of England. One of Ben's wealthier relatives owned sixty-three slaves; his immediate family owned eleven, including the Ned Waller slave family -- Ned and his wife, Celia, and their children Henry, Martha, Joe, Ned, Phillis, Winston, and Sarah.

The men of the Rawlings family were known for their great strength and fine physiques. Ben's grandfather, Richard Rawlings, "could hang a 56-pound weight on his little finger and write his name legibly at arm's length on the wall." His son and Ben's father, James Boswell Rawlings, was six feet, three and one half inches tall. With his long arms, he "could carry, on a wager, a barrel of flour under each arm up the mill steps." Ben Rawlings himself was over six feet tall. These men were well-suited to life in the deep countryside of western Spotsylvania, a land of rolling hills interlaced with numerous streams. Cleared land alternated with forests, where hunting was the primary entertainment of both men and boys. Horseback riding was a recreation as well as a necessity, and a fine horse properly equipped was coveted by all who could ride. One small boy was told that he must have "a pony and a little gun; and then your mother will always have plenty of game and you will have lots of fun."

Pasted upon this agricultural society, which emphasized physical strength and manly courage, was a thin veneer of chivalry, popularized by Sir Walter Scott's novels. In fact, some of Ben Rawlings' relatives suffered so acutely from what Mark Twain called the "Sir Walter disease" that they changed the name of the seventeenth century ancestral home from "Rawlingston" to "Ellangowan," the name of a manor house in Scott's novel, *Guy*

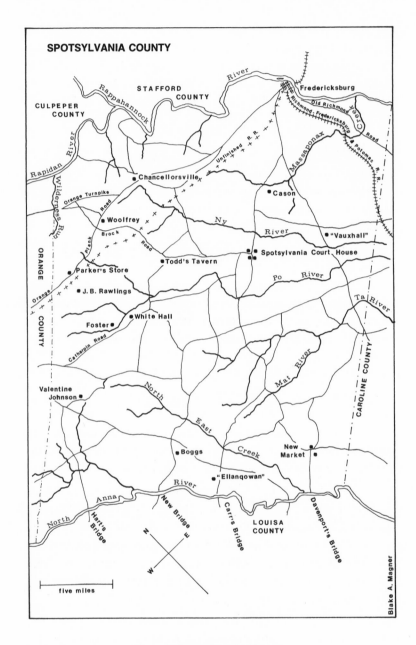

Map of Spotsylvania County

Map by Blake Magner.

Mannering. Tournaments in the style of *Ivanhoe* were extremely popular throughout the South, and Spotsylvania County was no exception. Beginning in the 1850's such contests were held yearly at the county fair. Costumed knights, with their elaborately caparisoned horses, heard a "charge" by the orator of the day and participated in various exercises of horsemanship. In 1860, participants in the county fair tournament were members of newly-formed militia companies, telling evidence of the grave threat of war.

Benjamin Rawlings thus grew up in a family which admired patriotic men who volunteered to serve their country. His cultural environment placed a premium upon personal bravery and physical courage; colorful tournaments presented combat as a manifestation of romantic, chivalric honor. Every segment of his environment persuaded Ben Rawlings to volunteer for the South.

The cultural images evoked by Ben Rawlings' story have led me to study ante-bellum Spotsylvania County, the Rawlings family genealogy records, literary and historical aspects of myth, and types of autobiography. Extensive historical reading and research in the Civil War period were necessary to verify the accuracy of Rawlings' statements and to provide explanatory notes and captions. His recollections proved to be remarkably accurate, although his memory perhaps was aided by the numerous Civil War articles in the family scrapbooks.

When Emery Rawlings wrote down his father's words in the third person, he omitted articles and used many abbreviations. Family tradition holds that Emery intended to put the Reminiscences in a more polished form, but he never did so. I have placed the Reminiscences in the first person, as Ben Rawlings dictated them, and hope that this latter day transcription has captured the flavor of Rawlings' dramatic oral history. I have corrected Emery Rawlings' minor spelling and punctuation errors and have written out the abbreviations. I have omitted a few short passages which were either unreadable or unclear. I have added a moderate number of sentences and connecting phrases to clarify the time sequence and flow of the story. The narrative of his prison experiences has been inserted in its logical place in the Reminiscences. The letters, notes, newspaper and scrapbook articles are all genuine; not a word in any of them has been changed. These materials, along with the Reminiscences, comprise the Rawlings Family Papers, owned by Rawlings' granddaughter, Florence Swift Durrance of Roswell, Georgia. These papers were the basis of my master's thesis in American Studies at the University of Miami, "Benjamin Rawlings: Confederate Archetype." The explanatory notes are based on the thesis footnotes and are well-documented. While the Reminiscences presented many problems of form, the story of Benjamin Rawlings' part in the truly epic event of his time is sufficiently compelling to warrant editorial corrections.

To Florence Swift Durrance I express my thanks for her kind generosity in allowing me to use the Rawlings Family Papers as a basis for my thesis and book. I received valuable help and advice from the late Dr. Meriwether Stuart of Yonkers, New York, professor emeritus of Hunter College; Dr. John F. Reiger of Ohio University, formerly of the University of Miami; the late George H. S. King of Fredericksburg, Virginia, a fellow of the American Society of Genealogists; and Robert K. Krick of Fredericksburg, Virginia, Chief Historian at the Fredericksburg-Spotsylvania National Military Park. My husband, James Emery Tribble, provided valuable assistance in matters of structure, concept, and logic. I sincerely thank all of my family and the many friends who have encouraged me to tell Ben Rawlings' story.

Byrd Barnette Tribble
Coral Gables, Florida
April, 1994

CHAPTER I

My Journey to Charleston

A few days after Christmas, 1860, I was visiting Uncle Ben Cason at his home, Mill Garden Farm, about six miles from Fredericksburg. I had been reading in the papers of the news from Charleston, and it seemed that war was about to start.[1] I was only fifteen, but I decided to go to Charleston without telling anyone, so I rode one of Uncle's horses into Fredericksburg and left it at the livery stable.

I had only six or seven dollars, but I took the train to Richmond, spent the night, and the next morning got on the train and rode to Weldon, North Carolina, which was as far as my money would take me.[2] I started from there afoot, and after walking two or three days, I got to Goldsboro, North Carolina, footsore and tired. I wrote home for money, but while waiting for it to come, I heard that the *Star of the West*[3] had been fired on, and being afraid they would fight before I arrived in Charleston, I decided to hurry on on foot.

I was soon sorry I had not waited for my money. It was cold and rainy the day I left Goldsboro, and that night I was very hungry and cold. I couldn't find many houses (I was following the railroad tracks) and the people at the ones I did find refused to keep me, so I kept walking until I got to a railroad trestle, which I was afraid to cross in the dark. Finally, I came to a Negro shanty by the track, where the Negro watchman allowed me to lie down and sleep until morning. The next morning, still without anything to eat, I started out over a dreary route across the swamps. The only food I had that day was a few raw turnips, which I dug out of a patch near the tracks. That night I came to an empty railroad car on a siding and slept in it for a while, but I woke up nearly frozen. It was so cold I thought it would be better to get up and start walking. After walking all the next day with nothing to eat, I came across a lumber camp that evening. The men were rough fellows, but they took care of me, giving me supper and breakfast, my first real meals since leaving Goldsboro.

1

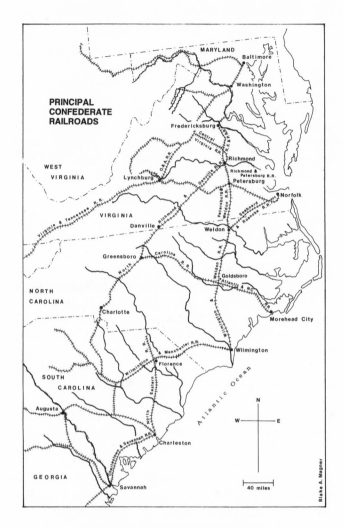

Map of Confederate Railroads

On his journey to Charleston, Ben Rawlings rode No. 6, the Richmond, Fredericksburg, and Potomac, to Richmond; No. 12, the Petersburg Railroad, to Weldon; and No. 34, the Northeastern Railroad, from Florence to Charleston.

Map by Blake Magner.

2

The next day and into the night I walked without food. About 11 P.M., cold and broken down,[4] I came to a small farm house occupied by Negroes. I woke them up and begged them to take me in but they declined. I was very cold and unable to go any farther, so I went into the barnyard and roused up first one cow and then the other, lying in their warm places. I kept this up until daylight, when I started out again in the drizzly rain. I was just about exhausted and starved and could find nothing to eat nor anyone to give me any food.[5]

Later that day, I crossed a bridge and came to a little station. By then I had concluded to try and "run my face." Boldly asking for a place to stay, I was directed to a house along the tracks, where I asked what they would charge as if I had coin. I got a fine supper and bed, and the next morning I ate an oversupply of breakfast to do for emergencies to come. I managed to slip away surreptitiously, leaving my host with the sack, but I got off O.K.

I walked all day, and toward night the rain came on again. Now I was in a better part of the state and came to a nice little village. Deciding to "run my face" again, I registered at a hotel, had a glass of wine, supper, a good bed, and breakfast. I felt good. My conscience hurt, so I left my top jacket with the proprietor as payment and went off down the tracks.

I kept up very well that day and ran across another little settlement. This place was called Florence. I had found out that cheek worked better than a tale of woe, so I went to a house, got supper, and asked for a bed. I was put in a room with a staid old preacher, and we were to bunk together, but the gospel cobbler[6] refused to share the bed. After some trouble I managed to get the bed for myself, but the next morning I had nothing to leave for payment. Seeing a bowling alley, I stood around and watched the games. Finally, a young, round-faced, jolly-looking planter noticed my youthful and disconsolate appearance and questioned me in a kindly way. I made a confidant of him, telling my story that I was on my way to Charleston to volunteer and that my money had run out. Out of his wholesome generosity, he told me he would see me through. He waited until the train came in, introduced me to the conductor, and had me franked through to Charleston.

I arrived in Charleston about daylight and started uptown sans friends or money. I decided to depend on my wits. I inquired for the best hotel and was sent to the Charleston Hotel. I registered in the office as if I owned the place and asked when breakfast would be ready. I got washed, brushed my hair, and went to the large dining room, which had white waiters. I ordered a first class breakfast but kept watching the waiters, afraid that someone would keep me from eating. After breakfast, I got a toothpick and went out into the lobby, feeling well-satisfied. Soon I met a gentleman and told him why I had come to Charleston. He took an interest in me and took me to meet John Preston,[7] a prominent old Virginian. Preston questioned me all about my background and then asked me about my financial condition. I told him that I was broke but that I was expecting money from home. He kindly took me to the Pavillion Hotel where he was staying. He told the proprietor that I was a Virginia friend of his and to let me have whatever I wanted or needed and to charge it all to him. He also promised to introduce me to officer friends of his when I wanted to go over to the island to join the troops. He would also send letters of introduction. I did not hurry to go, as I wanted a good rest and was in good quarters while waiting for money from home to come. Seeing all of the young men going into the hotel barber to be shaved, I went in and ordered a shave, which amused the colored barber. I got a clean face anyway.

Later that day, I met a fine-looking young man in a handsome uniform who, after hearing of my adventures, offered to show me the town. He took me to meet some lovely young ladies, and I met some high-ranking officers, Surgeon General Gibbs among them. Also, I was introduced to the famous Edmund Ruffin[8] as a fellow Virginian.

I wrote to Goldsboro to have my mail forwarded. Colonel Preston verified my identity so that the officials in Goldsboro would forward my money as well. It came a few days later along with a very affecting letter from Mother telling of when they found I was gone and they knew not where. My bills paid and my credit established, I felt very good.

Charleston Hotel

Photograph courtesy of Massachusetts Commandery Military Order of the Loyal Legion and the USAMHI.

JOHN PRESTON was the "prominent old Virginian" whom Rawlings met soon after he arrived in Charleston. He paid for Rawlings' hotel room, his military equipment, and introduced him to well-known South Carolinians. The influential Preston informed newspapers in South Carolina and Virginia of Rawlings' arrival to Charleston. When stories of the young Virginia volunteer appeared in print, Rawlings quickly became a local hero. (Newspapers at that time did not print what we think of as human interest stories; it was very rare for anyone other than a political or military leader to be the subject of a newspaper article.) Anxious for Virginia to secede, Preston hoped Rawlings' actions would help to edge Virginia public opinion toward secession. A Virginian educated at the University of Virginia and Harvard, he had made a fortune from his Louisiana sugar plantation. Preston was married to the sister of Wade Hampton, a wealthy South Carolinian who later headed Hampton's Legion of cavalry in the Army of Northern Virginia. At the beginning of the war, Preston was on the staff of General P. G. T. Beauregard and later headed the Bureau of Conscription. Preston and his family figure prominently in Mary Boykin Chesnut's *A Diary From Dixie*.

Photograph courtesy of Library of Congress.

The Charleston *Courier*
Monday morning, January 21, 1861
Page 2, Column 4

"Youthful volunteers. -- Benjamin C. Rawley [sic] Spotsylvania, Virginia, aged 16 years, was on a visit to Petersburg [sic], Va., when he heard of the occupation of Ft. Sumter and the probability of war against South Carolina. He immediately sent his horse home, and set out for Charleston, walking a great part of the way.

On his arrival here, and the report of his intention, Col. John S. Preston, generously undertook to equip him, and he is now awaiting response from him to be enrolled as a recruit under Lieut. W. Hampton Gibbes.

Columbus Daniel, 18 years of age, has reached the city from Nashville on a similar mission, and has been enrolled by Lieutenant Gibbes."

Fredericksburg *News*
February 5, 1861

A VIRGINIA YOUTH OF SIXTEEN IN THE SOUTH CAROLINA ARMY -- The Carolinian's correspondent furnishes the following:
"Among the interesting incidents which have occurred, is that of a youth of sixteen -- Benjamin Rawlings, of Virginia -- coming to volunteer. He was at Fredericksburg, about twenty miles from his home, when he heard of Fort Sumter being occupied by Anderson. He had not time to see his father, but sent his horse home and came off immediately. At Weldon his funds failed, and he walked to Florence -- on one day fifty-five miles. At this place he told his case to a conductor of the

Northeastern Railroad, who franked him to Charleston. Your correspondent [John Preston] sent him with a note to Col. Gregg and a request to allow him to join the Columbia Rifles, which he consented to on the condition that he should get his father's consent, which he has been anxiously awaiting. Today he had received it but yielded reluctantly, as his father says if South Carolina has fighting to do, Virginia will also have, and he would prefer him to join one of her companies. He has gone to consult Col. Gregg as to whether he will take him until Virginia needs him. He is a very intelligent youth and of the true "grit." Should he remain, he will be equipped by a patriotic citizen of Columbia."

Permission for Leave of Absence, Signed by Maxcy Gregg and Written by Alexander Cheves Haskell

Head Quarters Forces
Morris Island
24th February 1861

Private Benj. Rawlings of Company "A" has leave of absence for two weeks -- from the 25th February to 17th March. If his health is not restored by the end of that time, he will report by letter; and remain absent, until he receives an answer.

M Gregg
Col 1st Regt S. C. Vol.
Commanding on Morris Island

Letter from Richard H. Rawlings to Benjamin Rawlings, His Nephew

Grove Hill, Alabama
March 28, 1861

My Dear Nephew:

Yesterday I received a letter from Brother Ben, saying that you left home on the 24th of Dec. last & enlisted in the Army of South Carolina. I was not sorry to learn that you had become a soldier in defense of your native South, for I would have expected such conduct of one of your temperament; but I did regret that you had to suffer so much in getting to Charleston. Alas! that our old Mother Virginia has become so degenerate that her sons have to flee her borders to protect their honor and manhood.

You deserve great credit for the sacrifices you made to serve the South: and in this region [Alabama] you would be much appreciated for your conduct, but in Va. I fear such services would be considered a reproach rather than an honor -- judging from the debate in our Convention. I suppose you have enlisted in the Volunteer Corps of South Carolina for 12 mo., and not in the Regular Army of the Con. St. of America. If so, let me advise you not to go into the Regular Army -- I will give you my reasons for this advice when I hear from you.

When you are discharged from your Company, come to my house in Alabama and make it your home; I have no children and never expect to have any, and therefore will be ABLE to do something for you after a while; if you have any inclinations that way, you could *read law* with me, and after a while go into partnership with me. How would you like to be a lawyer?

9

Have you any present use for funds? My idea of a soldier's life is, that while in service, money is inconvenient to take care of, and that when he is discharged from the service he most needs it. *If you need it*, however, at present, *I will send you some.* If you will come on here when discharged, I will send funds to pay your expenses to this place.

Your affectionate uncle,
Richard H. Rawlings

CHAPTER II

Two Initiations

After several days, I decided it was time to get down to business and join a command, so Col. Preston gave me a letter of introduction for Col. Maxcy Gregg[1] of the First South Carolina Regiment, then on Sullivan's Island. I took the boat over to the island, called on Col. Gregg, and gave him the letter of introduction. He sent me to Capt. Mullins from Columbia, South Carolina, whose company had mostly college boys and the first blood of South Carolina. Capt. Mullins declined to enlist me until he had the consent of my father, so I returned to the city, wrote home, and in a short time got Pa's consent. Then I enlisted in Co. A,[2] Capt. Miller's company, one of considerable reputation, having served under Col. Gregg in the Mexican War.

I soon found that a soldier's life on the island was different from the city excitement. It was very hard at first, even though we were quartered in the summer residences of the well-to-do people of Charleston. Away out in the harbor we could see the Federal gunboats. We were armed with Enfield rifles, and it was great sport to fire at the buoys. We sank several.

We were finally sent to Morris Island[3] on the opposite side of the harbor. We took the boat over on a cold, snowy day, remarkable for that climate, and were quartered in tents near an old quarantine hospital. Morris Island was well-fortified with batteries of 32 Columbyards, which covered the channel so as to keep the gunboats from giving aid to the fort. These guns were fired for practice nearly every afternoon at the Yankee fleet, in sight yet out of range. I found to my surprise that I could see the ball after it left the gun. The noise was so great we had to hold our ears. We drilled constantly every day, mostly skirmish drill by the sound of the bugle.

Here I was challenged to fight a duel. In the Darlington Company, there was a lieutenant,[4] a self-sufficient brag and a great one to talk critically about Virginians. He made fun of F.F.V.'s,[5] saying he had never met a man from Virginia who was not an

11

Brigadier General Maxcy Gregg

Photograph courtesy of Massachusetts Commandery Military Order of the Loyal Legion and the USAMHI.

The Richland Rifles

The Richland Rifles, the South Carolina regiment which Ben Rawlings joined, are pictured on the left, as South Carolina governor Francis W. Pickens reviews the volunteer troops prior to the bombardment of Fort Sumter.

Photograph courtesy of Frank Leslie.

13

F.F.V., and I did not enjoy it. I discussed these insults with my messmates, who led me to believe that I must challenge the lieutenant on the field of honor. Feeling the honor of Virginia to be at stake and being the only one to defend it, I arranged for the challenge to be made. The messmates obligingly offered to arrange the preliminaries. They reported that the lieutenant had accepted the challenge and that we were to meet the next morning on the beach with our Enfield rifles. My messmates seemed to think I should be pleased at their success in arranging matters. I did not feel so good, as I began to think it might have been arranged without blood. Seeing no way out, I decided to fight and told my seconds I would be there on time. I felt quite serious and spent the rest of the day writing letters to my mother and friends. I made arrangements to have them mailed if the outcome was unfortunate. I retired on my straw pallet but did not sleep much. I had no idea of backing out, feeling as if the honor of the state was in my keeping. I thought I might die, but I would never show the white feather.[6] I could see all night in my mind a young Virginian, shot through, lying on the beach.

The next morning I was up bright and early, ready to be called on, with my Enfield rifle in good shape. Much to my surprise, I was not called to proceed to the field of honor. I could not understand why I was not called on at sunrise. I asked my seconds why the affair did not come off and was told that the company officers had gotten hold of it and if anything more was heard of it, I would be put in the guardhouse and that I had no right to challenge a commissioned officer. I felt very much relieved but did not show it to the seconds, complaining to them that I felt very much aggrieved and was anxious to have the affair come off. Then I saw the boys laughing and gathering around together and then commenced to smell a rat. Finally, they began to poke fun at me, and I found out I was the victim of a hoax.

Finally, around April 11, everything was prepared to open fire on Fort Sumter,[7] and an order came for expert riflemen from each flanking company to go down to Cummings Point, at the extreme end of the island about 1,300 yards from the fort. The riflemen, who were to pick off the soldiers manning the parapet guns on the fort, were to be volunteers and good shots. I volunteered at once, told some wonderful yarns about picking off

14

EDMUND RUFFIN, an extreme secessionist, was a Virginia agricultural reformer who had long advocated independence for the South. He attended the secession conventions in South Carolina, Florida, and North Carolina in an effort to persuade those states to leave the Union. Rawlings was introduced to Ruffin, most likely by John Preston, on one of the several occasions when Ruffin was in Charleston in the winter and spring of 1861. Here Ruffin is pictured in the uniform he wore as an honorary member of the Palmetto Guard, the artillery unit on Cummings Point at the tip of Morris Island.

Photograph courtesy of the National Archives.

squirrels in the Virginia woods, and got on the detail. We were marched down to Cummings Point the night before the firing commenced. I slept not much and wrote to Ma, saying that we expected the next day to be a bloody one and we did not know what the outcome would be.

The next morning before daybreak we were aroused and after a little while saw a signal gun from James Island, a mortar, go up through the air, making a beautiful curve in the darkness and exploding over the fort. Soon from the other side of the fort came another shot, either from Ft. Pinckney or Ft. Moultrie, which curved in the air and exploded over Sumter.[8] Then a half-dozen shots came from various places -- Morris, James, Moultrie, Pinckney -- all making a beautiful display of fireworks. The Columbyards from Moultrie, Morris, James, and the floating battery -- all the heavy guns began. We climbed on top of some of the batteries and could see the dust as solid shot hit the walls of the fort. The fort had not returned fire. There were four or five batteries on Morris Island, 1 mortar battery, 2 of heavy Columbyards, a railroad battery of railroad iron braced with palmetto logs, and a single rifled cannon, which had been presented to the citizens of Charleston by the citizens of Liverpool -- the first one of its kind used in the Civil War.

All at once, Fort Sumter opened fire with one of the big guns. We saw the puff of smoke and heard the shriek of solid shot that flew over our heads and ricocheted up in an arch behind us; we went for cover then. Then three or four guns opened on the batteries at Cummings Point, and guns on the other side of the fort fired at Moultrie and Pinckney. The parapet guns were so exposed that Anderson decided not to man them, so we were allowed to go about where we pleased during the firing. I slipped along from battery to battery before Anderson opened fire, seeing the results of our shots. I saw my old friend Edmund Ruffin mounted on a couple of barrels of sand looking over the battery. Anderson got the range pretty well after his third or fourth shot, and after a little while a big Columbyard hit the battery where Ruffin was standing, about the third palmetto log down, knocking logs and sandbags everywhere. The force of the concussions knocked Ruffin off and the next I saw of him he was scrambling up, covered with sand, and pulling for a healthier climate.[9] As the day wore away, I did not

16

mind it so much, as no one was killed. To get in the fight, several of us fired shots at the base of the fort, and afterwards flattened bullets were found there. The firing kept up for about thirty-six hours, and we expected the fleet to come to Anderson's assistance. We could see the shots were doing damage. On the second day the fire seemed to slacken, and finally I saw the white flag go up, and the Confederates ceased firing with cheering from all the troops. I saw Senator Wigfall[10] put off in a small boat from James Island. He went to the fort to arrange terms of capitulation.

About this time I ran across the captain of police from Charleston, whom I had met in the city. He seemed anxious to get over to the city to tell the news and asked me if I could handle an oar. I thought I could, so we jumped in a rowboat, but I was too excited to row properly, much to the disgust of the policeman. The boat turned round and round, and the policeman swore lustily. Then we heard shouting along the shore, and the boys said the fleet was coming up, so then we wanted to get back to the island. Finally I jumped out and pulled the boat ashore. I went to get under the cover of the batteries, but the boats never came in, and we were not fired on.

After arranging the surrender of the fort, Anderson was given the privilege of saluting the flag before taking it down. During the ceremony, one of his guns burst, killing three or four men, the only casualties of the fight. Anderson and his men were transferred to gunboats the next day, and the Confederates took possession of Fort Sumter.

Charleston *Courier*
January 12, 1861
Page 2, Column 3

Excerpt from Personal Sketches of Members of the South Carolina Convention by a correspondent of the Baltimore *American*.

> "Hon. Maxcy Gregg is a noted lawyer of recognized ability and legal acumen. He is most easily recognized on account of peculiarly constructed ear

17

LOUIS T. WIGFALL, a former United States senator and a native of South Carolina, was an early, ardent secessionist. On April 13, Rawlings saw Wigfall "put off in a small boat from James Island. He went to the fort to arrange terms of capitulation." On his own, Wigfall discussed surrender with Major Anderson. This peculiar action caused both Anderson and the authorized Confederate representatives great embarrassment. Wigfall and his wife are often mentioned in *A Diary From Dixie*.

Photograph courtesy of Library of Congress.

18

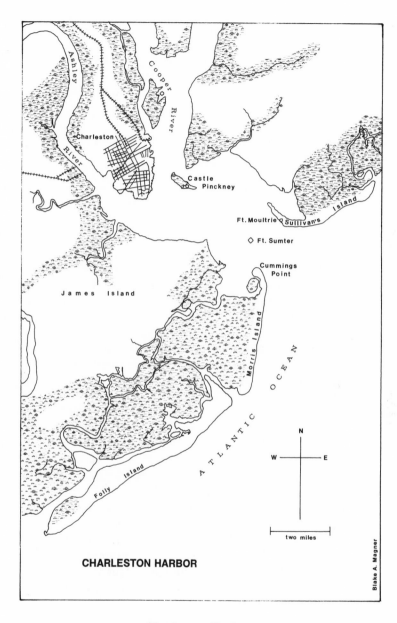

Charleston Harbor

Map by Blake Magner.

19

trumpets, which he uses on account of deafness. In manner, he is quick and nervous; is of a sanguine temperament, and speaks very fast. His face is remarkably good."

Letter from Richard H. Rawlings to Benjamin Rawlings, His Nephew

Grove Hill, Alabama
April 2, 1861

Dear Ben:

Your letter of the 17th inst. was received yesterday, and I answer at the earliest moment.

About ten days ago, I received a letter from Bro. Ben, saying that you had run off from home on the 26th of December last to enlist in the South Carolina Army; and the next day after receiving his letter, I wrote *you* a long letter and directed it to Charleston, South Carolina -- you will get the letter by inquiring at the Charleston post office.

Well, Ben, I hardly know what to advise you to do, unless I could talk with you upon the subject; I do not think you would be satisfied with the army after a little while; the sacrifices are so great and numerous that you probably would reject it. My advice to you, however, is to choose that profession to which your inclinations lead you -- whether it be soldier, merchant, or lawyer; this is necessary to success. If you conclude to remain in the army, I will do all I can for you at Montgomery towards promotion. If you wish to be a lawyer, my office and books are at your service; I have, you know, about $1,500 worth of law books which would be of much assistance to you in studying law, and will charge you nothing for their use or for directing your studies. If your father agrees to it, I will make this arrangement with you: I will pay one half of all your expenses here including board, clothes, pocket money, etc., which would be about $250 per annum; board alone would be $180 per annum and I would charge you nothing for instructing you, and pay one half of the $250 per annum if your father will pay the other half. But I do not wish to be understood as persuading you to study law; you must choose your profession yourself; Law is a science, & requires severe labor and intense application from her votaries before she vouchsafed success; but at the same time she promises to the diligent an ample reward. After mature reflection, and after consultation with your father, (for he has your interest more at heart than any other man on the earth) choose your profession; and if you determine upon studying law, take my proposition under consideration. But whatever you determine upon, I shall be glad to render you any aid in my reach.

I am glad you volunteered at the time you did, & hope there will be no necessity for resorting to the arbitrament of the sword to settle the present difficulty.

At any rate, you must come and see me when you are discharged. I would not remain in the army longer than July, unless I determined to make arms my profession; but I would advise you to serve out your time until July, no matter what you determine upon. Write to me often. I am doing very well here in the practice of law.

Your affectionate uncle,
Richard H. Rawlings

Letter of Richard H. Rawlings to James Boswell Rawlings, His Brother and Benjamin Rawlings' Father[11]

Grove Hill, Alabama
April 3, 1861

Dear Brother:

As I have not heard from you and family for a long time, I write for the purpose of showing you that I have not forgotten you, and to learn what you are doing in old abolitionized Virginia. Don't you think all hands of the Rawlings family had better move to Texas? I am doing very well here, but I know "there is a better land" in the South-West, Texas; and if I could get you all started there I would pull up stakes here and go with you; but this country is far ahead of Va., and Clarke County is the poorest part of Alabama. You all that own Negroes ought to get out of Va.; if I owned Negroes now in Va. I would either sell them for whatever they would bring, or move them to the Cotton states; there never was a *brighter* future before a Confederacy than that of ours;[12] we do not fear the world in arms; our people are united and would to-day vote one-half of their wealth, if necessary, to maintain their present position. But I must write you of Ben: I received a letter from him by last mail from Charleston, asking my advice as to what course he should pursue -- whether choose *the Camp for life or some civil pursuit.* I wrote him a very candid letter, & told him to write you on this subject, as a father could be relied on more than anyone else; told him to consult his own inclinations in choosing a profession; for it would be useless to attempt to be eminent in anything unless one's heart is set upon it.

I wrote him that if, after mature reflection, and after consulting with you, he wished to study law, I would be glad to afford him any assistance in my power; would charge him nothing for the use of my libraries, not for instruction in a course of legal study; that his expenses here for board, clothing, pocket money, etc., would be about $250 per annum, and that I would pay one-half of these expenses, if he wished to read law -- provided you sanctioned his studying law and would pay the other half. I would like to advise Ben what to do, without regard for anything I may write; for I am unwilling to take the responsibility of advising him to choose this or that profession; while at the same time I would say nothing to discourage him if he inclined that way of his own accord. So that while I would be glad to render *any* assistance to Ben I can, I am unwilling to take the responsibility of recommending him to read law. My own experience is that the same application and industry devoted to any other pursuit, pays better than the law; only about one lawyer in ten makes anything clear of his expenses; I am now barely paying mine -- though I commenced too late in life to read Law; and therefore, if Ben has any inclination to try the Law, now is the time for him to commence laying the foundation. Let me hear your views upon this subject -- probably they harmonize with mine. I suppose Zack is married -- I heard he was to be married, but never heard whether he was or not. I don't get much news these days from home. Why don't Nannie write to us sometimes, and Lucy too. I think they might, if they too are not married. My love to all.[13]

Yours affectionately,
R. H. Rawlings

Charleston *Courier*
April 1, 1861
Page 1, Column 4

Excerpt from THE VISIT TO THE FORTIFICATIONS [by members of the South Carolina Convention and other dignitaries.]

[The Richland Rifles] "went through the manual in a short time, marching in quick and double time; forming platoons; charging, loading and firing etc., with great unanimity of action. The military display of all the companies exhibited thorough drilling, the most rigid discipline, and made a very favorable impression on the minds of visitors."

CHAPTER III

I Return Home to Virginia

After the surrender, I went back to my regiment at our Morris Island camp. I read the papers and could see the excitement caused by the firing on Fort Sumter and the effect on Northerners. A short while afterwards, I was on duty walking the beat in front of the guardhouse, when our adjutant came galloping by. He recognized me and told me that Virginia had seceded;[1] I threw up my hat and had a big celebration all to myself.

A few days afterwards, it was circulated in camp that South Carolina troops would be sent to Virginia, as that would be the seat of the war. Very much to my surprise, I found that few of the soldiers wanted to go to Virginia.[2] They would have to volunteer again, as they were only enlisted to fight in the state for six months. Finally the regiment was called out in parade, and Col. Gregg made a speech in which he told us that the fighting would be in Virginia and called for volunteers to go. All volunteers were to step four paces to the front. Much to the Colonel's chagrin, hardly one-eighth of the regiment stepped forward. Finally he rode up to our company and said in surprise, "Is this all of the old Richland Rifle Company who will volunteer to go to the succor of old Virginia?" At this, about one-half of the company stepped forward; finally, after much pleading, about two-thirds of the First Regiment, South Carolina Volunteers, did step out.

In a few days we received our marching orders; we packed up and went over on the boat to the city to take the train for Virginia. We were held there until the next day, so we stacked our guns and went off in the city, got a good meal, and roamed around with not much discipline. I had packed a lot of palmetto leaves to take home to friends as mementoes; I had them all in my knapsack, which I had left with our guns on the wharf. When we got ready to go, I found someone had stolen all of my things, clothes and all.

Our trip from Charleston to Virginia was a perfect ovation. We were the first troops to go through from the South. Big crowds cheered us at all the towns; when we stopped and went in stores to buy, the merchants would not take our money. There was a big ovation when we got to Richmond, and we were feted and made a great deal of as the first troops to come to Virginia.[3] Discipline was not strict: we could go to the city, take meals, and even spend the night in town.

I neglected to mention that before we left Charleston and after the firing on Fort Sumter, I was in the city on a pass. A young fellow came up to me who could speak only broken English. He was a Pole named Stobowski who claimed to be one of the nobility. He seemed to have found out about me and wished to join my company. He applied a few days later and went with us to Virginia. "Ski" talked big, and the boys did not like him very much and were a little suspicious of him. At Richmond, a high-spirited messmate named Treadwell had a big fuss with him and challenged "Ski" to a duel. He accepted the challenge, and the two were to fight the next morning at sun-up on the back part of the fairgrounds. Treadwell was there, but "Ski" wasn't. Treadwell was so angry that he got a stick, hunted "Ski" up, and thrashed him. Some months later, "Ski" deserted during the Peninsula Campaign.

After we had been in camp around Richmond for a while, I began to get homesick and finally got a ten day pass home. I borrowed money to go. I took my rifle and went to Orange Court House and got a horse from Uncle Ben Rawlings and then went by Uncle Herndon Frazier's house.[4] It was a warm day, so I took off my coat, strapped it behind my saddle, and with my gun on my back, I was certain that I was the cynosure of all eyes. A bridge near our house was washed away, so I jumped a fence and swam some distance above the crossing and came back to the road. Some Negroes saw me and told a big yarn about a wild, red-shirted man swimming the river on a horse. I finally got home and Ma was glad to see me.

I found the whole countryside in excitement -- companies were being formed and everyone was drilling. Ma and Pa wanted me to join a company from our own county; the idea suited me as I felt like I could get a promotion as an old veteran in a green company. I finally met with Capt. Johnson[5] of the old Mt. Pleasant Rifle Company, whose company was being mustered in at the Fredericksburg fairgrounds. Capt. Johnson was very anxious to get me in his company and offered me the position of Orderly Sergeant with the prospect of a commission.

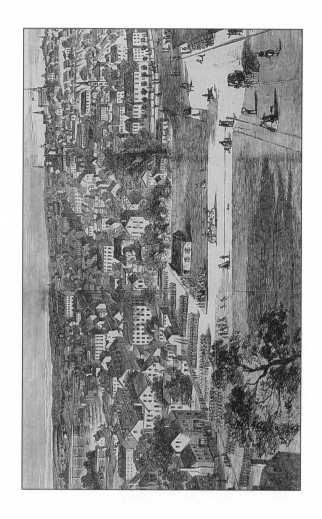

Early Volunteers Parading in Richmond

When the First South Carolina Volunteers reached Richmond, they were "feted and made a great deal of as the first troops to come to Virginia."

*Illustration from **Battles and Leaders.***

27

I returned to Richmond, applied to Col. Gregg, and he game me my transfer to the Mt. Pleasant Rifle Company.[6] I did not ask any questions but took my Enfield rifle with me and kept it as long as I carried a gun. I reported for duty at the Fredericksburg fairgrounds.

From the Virginia *Herald*
April 27, 1861

TROOPS FROM SOUTH CAROLINA

Brigadier General M. D. Bonham, at the head of five hundred troops from South Carolina, arrived in Richmond on Wednesday evening by the Southern train. Every man of them looked a hero; dark and sunburnt from exposure, their countenances lighted up with martial ardor, their fine physique, their perfect equipments, all denoted an invincible and heroic race of men.

Among them was our young friend and countryman, Rawlings, son of Mr. Benj. [sic] Rawlings. Young Rawlings was so enthused that he left his father's house unknown, over four months since, repaired to Charleston, enlisted at once, and was on Morris Island during the bombardment and capture of Fort Sumter. He is about 18 [sic] years of age, and is a worthy representative of Old Spotsylvania.

From the Fredericksburg *News*

"Young Rawlings" of Spotsylvania, who volunteered to join the soldiers of South Carolina and was at Morris Island during the bombardment of Fort Sumter, we had the pleasure of meeting yesterday. He has the modesty of youth and worth, and we hope will enjoy his furlough among his friends in town and county. A hearty welcome to him.

From Col. Maxcy Gregg to Benjamin Rawlings

Camp Pickens, 10 May 1861

My young friend

      I have received this evening your letter of May 8 -- and now enclose the honorable discharge requested.
      With my best wishes for your promotion and success, and for your good father's welfare, I remain

Sincerely your friend
Maxcy Gregg

to Mr. Benjamin C. Rawlings
Fredericksburg, Spotsylvania County, Virginia

Letter of Discharge from Col. Maxcy Gregg

Headquarters 1st Regt. So. Ca. Vol.
Camp Pickens, near Richmond
10 May 1861

Private Benjamin C. Rawlings, of Company A is hereby, with the consent of Captain D. B. Miller, commanding the company, honorably discharged from the service.

On the news of the approach of hostilities, without waiting to ask his Father's consent (which he was confident would be given), he hurried to Charleston in January last, and applied to me to receive him into my Regiment, then guarding Sullivan's Island. From his youth, but being sixteen years old as he told me, I declined to receive him until he could hear from his Father. But he obtained a promise from me, that if a fight commenced before he could receive an answer from his Father, I would not refuse to receive him into the ranks. With his Father's approbation, he entered Captain Miller's Company, and served in the ranks well and faithfully until after the arrival of the Regiment in Virginia. He was with the Regiment on Morris Island during the bombardment of Fort Sumter. As he desires now to enter in to service of his native state, I have consented, in accordance with a promise which I made him first, to discharge him for that purpose. I think he well deserves a Commission, notwithstanding his youth. If I had a Lieutenancy at my disposal, I would most cheerfully offer it to him. He has evinced a high spirit which I have admired, as well as a faithful attention to duty. And he has been trained in an exceedingly well drilled Rifle Company.

The above discharge to date from 2 May 1861.

Maxcy Gregg
Col. 1st Regt. So. Ca. Vol.

CHAPTER IV

Growing Up in the Army

Captain Johnson gave me the position of Orderly Sergeant, but I soon found I knew nothing about the job. I could not keep an accurate roll at first. I would get things all mixed up, and the boys would laugh at me and give me different names each time I tried to untangle things. Often I would go back to my tent, lie down, and cry at night. But I stuck to it.

At first, we could go to Fredericksburg and get something good to eat and have a good time. Then came rumors that the enemy was sending gunboats up the Rappahannock. Our company was sent into camp along the river.[1] The oyster boats came up the river, so we had plenty to eat, but it got to be very lonesome. I was used to being around town, so it went very hard with me. I could not get a pass, so I decided to take French leave,[2] intending to get back before morning. In town, I heard that our regiment had been ordered back to town, so I foolishly thought I could wait and join the regiment in town and save myself a trip back to camp. Of course, I was reported absent without leave and was arrested. I was put in the guardhouse in a little upper story of the courthouse at Fredericksburg. I was very much mortified and chagrined, and being a non-commissioned officer, I belatedly saw what a serious offense it was. After a few days, I was sent back to camp (the regiment was now at the fairgrounds), but I was still under arrest.

Soon after this came orders to go to Aquia Creek, where the enemy was rumored to be. Captain Johnson came up to me, very excited, and offered to relieve me from arrest for a while. He was anxious to have me with the company if we were to be under fire as I was the only experienced enlisted man. I made Captain Johnson promise not to bring the charges up again, so I took my old place and went to camp on Aquia Creek. The rumors proved to be a false alarm, but we stayed at Aquia Creek to support the batteries that were being built there. We camped on the old Tump fishing grounds,[3] where we could see the boats going by. One of them, the *Pawnee*, a large wooden boat, would fire an occasional shot to keep things exciting.

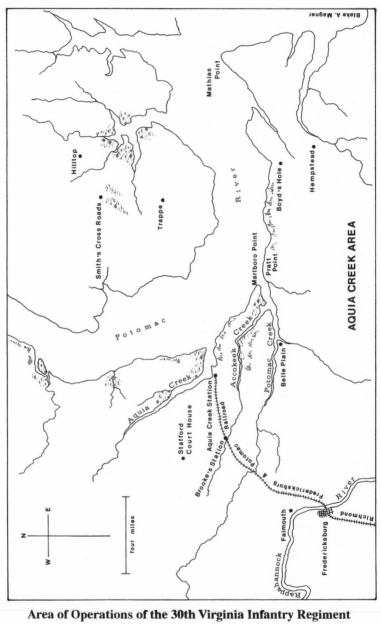

Mathias
Point

R i v e r

Hilltop •

Smith's Cross Roads •

Trappe •

Hempstead •

Boyd's Hole •

Pratt
Point

Marlboro Point

AQUIA CREEK AREA

P o t o m a c

Accokeek Creek

Potomac Creek

Belle Plain •

Aquia Creek

Stafford
Court House •

Aquia Creek Station

Brooke's Station

Railroad

P o t o m a c

Fredericksburg &

River

Richmond

N

E

W

four miles

Rappahannock

Falmouth •

Fredericksburg •

Area of Operations of the 30th Virginia Infantry Regiment

Map by Blake Magner.

32

Here we drilled every day. We got hold of *Hardee's Tactics* and drilled our squad until we began to get well-posted.

All of us wanted to catch some fish, so I got permission to take several men up Aquia Creek. While we were fishing some distance up the creek, the gunboats began shelling.[4] A shell would come singing over us, and the men were scared. I would reassure them, saying, "That's all right." When the shells came closer, I told them when to duck and convinced them that it was great sport. We came back to camp as fast as we could and got there about the time the firing ceased. Sergeant Rawlings made quite a reputation for himself for bravery under fire.

The next day, the *Pawnee*, reinforced by three or four other boats, took position in front of our camp, shelling the batteries and the woods in the rear where the troops were thought to be camped.[5] We were all called under arms and taken behind some hills where we would be protected. The boys were all excited this time. I was about one mile from camp when the firing commenced. I started back for camp, and a shell came over and exploded near me. Coming through the woods, I met a man from Company F from Richmond. We were nearly three miles from the boats, but this man was very excited with a Colt five shooter already cocked and yelling, saying the Yankees were landing. I got back to camp and found the company in line behind the hills. A shell came over now and then and exploded in the rear. The boys were all excited and looking for a battle; Captain Johnson and the other officers were about as excited as the men. I felt serene, knowing the danger to be small, so I took one of the men and went out to look for strawberries. We got plenty. The rest of the command looked upon us with holy horror as if we were tempting providence by our indifference to the bombardment. Towards night, the boats drew off with no damage being done.

Soon we were moved a few miles down to Marlboro Point[6] at the mouth of Potomac Creek. Here all of our companies were thrown together, and we practiced regimental and battalion drill. Then came a report that the Yankees were landing at Mathias Point, and we were ordered by forced march to that place. We crossed Potomac Creek in flatboats and started toward Mathias Point. It was a very hot day, and we made our first acquaintance

**Bombardment of Confederate
Batteries at Aquia Creek.**

The *Pawnee* and the *Freeborn* attack at Aquia Creek.

Photograph courtesy of Library of Congress.

34

with hardtack. It was a little mouldy, and none of the boys would eat it. Someone said it had been baked during the Mexican War. Four years later, we would have been glad to have that hardtack. We marched several miles and then were ordered back to camp. We were terribly exhausted after a march that would have been small a year or so later.

Company H, a Caroline County company under Captain Gouldin, was stationed at Mathias Point. This company, known as the Sparta Grays, was organized before the war and was armed with Sharps rifles. When the Yankee gunboats came up too close, Company H opened fire, killing the captain of one of the boats. This was about the first casualty on the Potomac River. The famous Purcell Battery from Richmond joined us here.

An epidemic of measles broke out in camp,[7] and I had them. I was sent to the hospital in Fredericksburg, but when Ma heard of it, she came with the carriage and took me out to Mill Garden, Uncle Ben Cason's place. In the meantime, my command marched up to Manassas as reinforcements to Beauregard against McDowell.[8] While I was sick with the measles, I could hear the guns at the first battle of Manassas [July 21], and I was very anxious to be there. After three or four weeks, I returned to the regiment, now at our old campgrounds at Marlboro Point. We stayed there until late in the fall of 1861, when we moved up about two miles in the rear of Aquia Creek.

CHAPTER V

Twenty-three Barrels of Cider

At Aquia Creek, we had our first experience with winter quarters.[1] We were issued round tents, which we improved upon by digging out a foundation four or five feet deep in the side of a hill and stretching the tent over it. Then we dug a fireplace in the side next to the hill and ran a little tunnel up the hill to take the smoke out. That answered as a chimney. Many of us got boxes of food from home, and we had a fairly good time.

We had a regimental sutler whose tent was outside camp on top of a steep hill. He always kept a good supply of food, but his prices were very high, and the boys were down on him. He had gotten in 23 barrels of cider and had put the barrels just outside of his tent. Four or five of the boys went in the sutler's tent and spread out in front of the counter, engaging his attention while others got behind the tent and shoved the barrels down the hill. Strange to say, they did not break. The sutler tried to find out who had done it and got very hot, threatening to report the affair to the colonel. But no one would tell, so the sutler persuaded about a dozen of the boys to go to the bottom of the hill and roll the barrels up, promising them a treat. Our crowd stood on top of the hill and chaffed them, calling to them to roll hard. When those boys came to be treated, the ones who had rolled the barrels down lined up first and got cigars and cider, while the boys behind (the ones who had rolled the barrels up) did not get any. We were puffing on our cigars and told the sutler about it, but he refused to come up again.

We stayed at this same camp a few months and had a very good time. Here we started the famous expression of "Found your mule,"[2] which we hollered at strangers coming in to camp, even officers. None of our own officers could ever find out who had done it because as soon as one fellow stopped yelling, another one away off would repeat it.

Along about the middle of the winter, large bodies of troops were arriving around Fredericksburg. Orders came for my company and Company F to go to Fredericksburg and act as Provost Guard. Some of us were quartered in the courthouse and the rest in old warehouses around in town. One man in my company had an aunt living in town, so we furnished the provisions and she cooked them. Occasionally, we were even allowed to sleep at her house in comfortable beds. We only had to report for roll call in the morning.

We received our regular pay, but the attractions in town kept us broke nearly all the time. A theatrical troop from Richmond came to town and we saw the Sally Partington Sisters.[3] We sang "Maryland, My Maryland" for the first time at the theater.

There were a great many troops from the far South camped near Fredericksburg. When they came into town, they kept the provost very busy, fighting and shooting nearly every night. On one occasion, I was going back to the barracks at the courthouse along with Tom Massy, a messmate, when he heard a terrible crashing of glass. We looked across the street, and there was a fellow smashing lanterns in front of the Presbyterian Church. He was a big, fierce-looking fellow, and when we tried to halt him, he ran his hands in his pockets. I thought he was going to draw a weapon, so I clinched him and called for Tom to help. So holding his arms, one apiece, we got him across the street towards the guardhouse. He never said a word, but just as he got across the street, he freed his right arm from Tom and hit him a whack right on the nose, which nearly knocked him down. But Tom recovered, hit the fellow back as hard as he could, and grabbed him again. I had managed to hold on all along. We hustled him over to our guardhouse and turned him over to the lieutenant of the guard. He turned out to be from Spotsylvania County, a man named Scott, who became a good soldier and who is now practicing medicine in Culpeper County.

CHAPTER VI

First Lieutenant at Seventeen

Along towards spring, our twelve-month enlistment was about over, and we were expecting to get home for a good time, when all at once bad news came from the West. Fort Donelson had fallen with a great number of men captured and killed. The governor asked all of us to re-enlist for three years or the war; a great many did but it was against the grain. When we were promised a thirty day furlough, nearly all of us re-enlisted. I went to my home in the county and was having a fine time on my furlough. When it was about half over, orders came to report to camp, where I found everyone blue from the reverses our armies had suffered. Enlistments all over the country expired soon, and it looked as if the army would be depleted. The Confederate Congress decided to hold the troops, requiring them to re-enlist or be conscripted. By then I had already re-enlisted.[1]

Toward the end of March, we were ordered to North Carolina to protect the railroad lines from the Yankees, who had captured New Bern. We went by train as far as Goldsboro, and again I had my knapsack and all my clothes stolen at the depot. At Camp McIntosh near Goldsboro, we were brigaded with three other regiments. In May, our regiments were re-organized, and we elected company and regimental officers. I got first lieutenant, and the new captain was Will Day. Lieutenant Colonel Archer Harrison got Colonel; the old colonel, R. Milton Carey was not elected. He was a good drill man but he had no stomach for fighting. All the new officers had to pass an examination. I stood mine with credit, but several failed.

Toward the end of May, we were ordered back to Petersburg[2] and from there, Company D and Company F were detailed to City Point, about twelve miles below Petersburg at the junction of the James and Appomattox.[3] We were to prevent the Yankee troops from landing off of the gunboats. We found City Point deserted, people fearing a Yankee landing or bombardment. Many houses, some of them beautiful residences, had been just left open.

Lieutenant General Theophilus Hunter Holmes

Photograph courtesy of Library of Congress.

Major General John G. Walker

Photograph courtesy of Library of Congress.

We were encamped about three miles from City Point back into the county. We kept pickets at the point to watch the gunboats. The rainy weather continued, sogging everything. I was quartered in an old tobacco barn. The dirt floor had become mud, and it was hard to find a dry place to lie down. I got a board about twelve inches wide and lay on the board across the beams, which were ten or twelve feet from the floor. I was liable to fall at the least turn in my sleep.

One night around one or two o'clock I was roused by one of the guards, calling me to come down right quick. I had to get my clothes on up there on the board and swing down to the ground. I found big excitement in camp. Everything was dark; all fires and lanterns were out. Brumley,[4] one of the pickets, had brought in a prisoner. He reported that he had started from his post with Harris, another picket, and another prisoner. The other prisoner had stabbed Harris, whom Brumley had been obliged to leave along the edge of the railroad tracks while he brought his prisoner in. I was ordered to send a detail of a corporal and four men to bring the wounded man to camp. We found Harris with six or seven wounds in his breast and arms, near death from loss of blood. We carried him on a stretcher to our regimental surgeon, and sent for whiskey.

Now it was necessary to get word to City Point so as to have the other pickets search for the escaped prisoner. I called for volunteers, but no one was anxious to go; the boys had lost their nerve after this accident. So, although I was now a commissioned officer, I volunteered to go. I started out through the Egyptian darkness[5] not able to see six inches. Then a big storm came up with sheet lightning so bright and often that I could see the ties on the railroad at every step. I had only my sword and a small pistol, which I kept cocked, expecting to meet the escaped prisoner. A stray dog in the woods caused me nearly to fire. After one and one-half miles, I came across the first pickets, a sergeant and three men at a crossroad. They were so nervous they nearly fired on me.

Here I got a first hand account of the trouble from Sergeant Johnson. Near the crossroad, a sentinel saw two men come blundering in from the bushes and arrested them. One seemed to be a sailor. The sergeant foolishly neglected to search them but put each one in the charge of a picket and started them to camp. Brumley, who was not more than fifteen years old, kept his in front of him at the muzzle of his gun, but Harris let his prisoner walk by his side and talk to him. After a short distance, this sailor, a big, strong fellow, all at once threw his left arm around Harris, grabbed his gun, stabbed him seven or eight times in the breast and shoulder, and ran back into the bushes. Brumley was just a few feet ahead of Harris, but it was too dark for him to help, so he kept marching and left Harris there by the railroad. I went on to City Point, notified the pickets, and then came on back, reaching camp just before daylight, very tired.

The next day some of the cavalry ran across the escaped prisoner in the woods and arrested him, putting him on a horse behind a cavalryman to send him to camp. As soon as the two were out of sight of the other men, the Yankee jerked the cavalryman's pistol out of the holster, knocked him on the head, and took off for the bushes again. He was never seen afterwards. The two were supposed to be spies sent from the boats and no doubt they got back that night. Harris was sent to the hospital and finally after a long time recovered and served the rest of the war. He is now a successful merchant in Fredericksburg but still carries scars on the breast and arms.

Excerpt from Journal of Lizzie Maxwell Alsop, Age Sixteen, Fredericksburg, Virginia

May 25, 1862

..."Aunts Dorry & Eliza were in town yesterday. The former told me that amongst the acquaintances formed while our Army was stationed near them, was Uncle Edward Barton's step son. He proved to be an exceedingly nice man. During the course of the conversation he happened to speak of Rawlings who formerly belonged to his company. Aunt Eliza recognizing the name said that Ben Rawlings from her county had joined a company from South Carolina at the commencement of the war, and upon "comparing notes" found that they were both speaking of the same individual. Mr. ----- pronounced Ben one of the bravest men in the world and the "noblest of Creation." I am glad that he is winning for himself laurels in the opinions of his countrymen. Ben Rawlings was my first lover when I was a school girl. Although he is only 17 or 18 and commenced fighting for his country as a private, he is now first Lieutenant in the "Mount Pleasant Rifles." May he continue to advance slowly but surely through life, till he at last shall have reached the highest pinnacle of military fame in this country." ...[6]

CHAPTER VII

Marching Around the Peninsula

We had been at City Point only a few days when the Battle of Seven Pines[1] began. We were ordered up to reinforce the army near Richmond. We got into Richmond about 4 A.M. and waited on the street until about 8 or 9 A.M., when we were ordered to march toward the battlefield. While waiting in Richmond, a large number of the men had gotten filled with whiskey before breakfast. When we got out of the city, men commenced falling out, and when we went into camp, nearly half were between Richmond and camp, gloriously drunk. Most of them came up that evening, but the fighting was all over and we did not get under fire.

We returned to camp near Petersburg and remained there quietly until the Seven Days[2] battles began. Again we were ordered north of the James and were sent down near Malvern Hill, where McClellan had taken a last stand under the gunboats. It was very hot and before getting down near the fighting we were marched and countermarched for nearly a week until all of us were very much exhausted and disgusted. One day we passed by the Gaines Mill battlefield, where my old South Carolina regiment had fought two days before. They had charged the New York Zouaves, and many on both sides were dead. The corpses were black from the great heat of the past two days.

The captain of Company D was away, so I was in command. At the right of the company was a large, reckless-looking character who was thoroughly exhausted by the heat and fatigue. He said he wished a bombshell would come and blow him to hell as he preferred being in hell to marching up and down that country. I was impressed by the fervor of his words.

We were then ordered down to a strip of woods about a mile and a half from the river and not one quarter of a mile from thirty guns that were placed on a hill.[3] We marched by the right flank down this strip of woods to the river to keep the enemy from finding our location. We had gone but a short distance when the gunboats opened fire; they seemed to get our exact location.[4] The shots came through the woods, and the first one exploded to the right of my company. I was at the head of the company but in front and to the left. One shot hit Wilson, the man who preferred hell to marching up and down the country. The hit took his heel, part of his foot, and tore flesh from his buttocks. He died that night. He got his wish very soon.

Now we halted and were ordered to get under cover. The gunboats kept shelling, and then the battery in front of us opened with the thirty guns. This was the worst artillery fire I ever experienced.[5] I happened to be near a very big white oak tree and I and several others got behind it, but we seemed to be between the devil and the deep blue sea. We would get behind the tree to get away from one shell in front, when from the right flank a gunboat shell of large size would come along, so we jumped from side to side as the shells came from side to side. While I was dodging the shells, I saw my second lieutenant doing the same thing, his face pale and his eyes rolling, and he looked so ludicrous that I got to laughing and could not control myself, and I just laughed and roared and the more I laughed, the scareder I got. I looked up the hollow and saw Colonel Harrison of our regiment behind a tree taking a big drink out of a flask, and he looked so scared that I laughed all the more. The boys all looked at me as if they thought I had gone crazy. This fire lasted until dark, when we marched back to where we had started that afternoon.

The next day, there was heavy fighting to the left of us,[6] and the Confederates there, including some Texans, were charging the batteries. The rifle fire sounded like sticks breaking in the woods. We were expecting orders to charge the batteries, too, but providentially they did not come, and we withdrew that night back from under fire. General Lee did not renew the attack on account of the gunboats, so we established a strong picket line and withdrew a few miles to the rear.

CHAPTER VIII

First Confederate in Harper's Ferry

About the middle of August,[1] we got orders to take up a line of march north. Jackson had already started.[2] Before we reached Orange Court House, the battle of Cedar Run had already been fought, and there Jackson wiped up on the braggart Pope, who had taken command a short while before, saying his headquarters were in the saddle. We went over the battlefield a few days after the fight and continued our march to the field of Second Manassas, which was over before we arrived.[3] Then we started for Maryland, crossing the Potomac at Leesburg.[4]

The ford at Leesburg was deep, and it was hard to keep on our feet. Some of the men were washed downstream. Then we went on into Maryland and crossed the Monocacy River, where we awaited an engagement for several days. We were instead sent back to the Potomac to destroy the Chesapeake and Ohio Canal aqueduct over the Monocacy. Unfortunately, our explosives were not strong enough to blow up the stone bridge, so we then were ordered back into Virginia to Harper's Ferry. The water was very cold when we crossed at Point of Rocks at night. We marched on in the rear of Loudoun Heights and took position at the foot of the mountain. Jackson had already invested Harper's Ferry. Batteries were ordered to be placed on the top of Loudoun Heights.[5] My company was in camp at the eastern base of the mountain; we could hear the firing but could see nothing. Finally, I couldn't stand it any longer, so I left my company in the command of the second lieutenant and without permission took one of the men and climbed up on the mountain to see. We got to the top and ran across Cooke's Battery of our brigade. They were firing down on Harper's Ferry. About 100 yards to the left was a large stone enclosure. There I saw Captain French and General Walker, the brigade commander. They were behind a stone wall and pretty safe. At the top of Loudoun Heights, I found a splendid spectacle: just below us and across the river was the town of Harper's Ferry, while to the right and across the Potomac was Maryland Heights, also surmounted by a battery which was firing into the town about 1,500

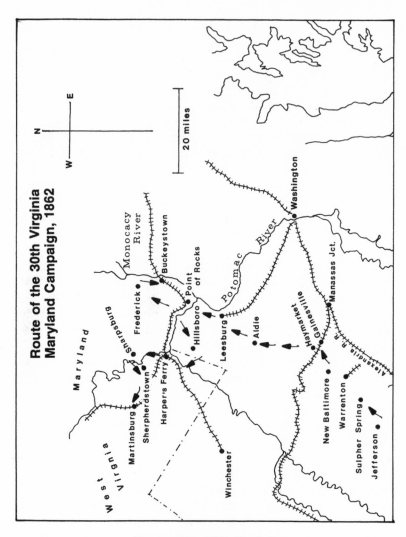

Route of the 30th Virginia
Maryland Campaign, 1862

Map by Blake Magner.

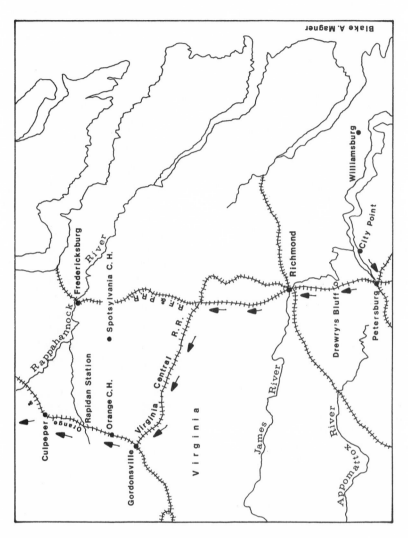

**Route of the 30th Virginia
Maryland Campaign, 1862**

Map by Blake Magner.

47

Description of the Route of the 30th Virginia

August 20: from City Point to Drewry's Bluff

Camped near Richmond until August 26, when regiment took train to Rapidan Station

Camped on Orange side of Rapidan River until September 1, when the regiment marched to one mile north Culpeper

September 2: marched to Jefferson

September 3: crossed Rappahannock, passed through Fauquier Springs (also seen on maps as Sulphur Springs) and Warrenton; camped 4 miles past Warrenton on Warrenton Turnpike

September 4: passed through New Baltimore, Buckland, and Gainesville, where they camped and visited the Second Manassas Battlefield

September 5: marched through Haymarket, Aldie and to within 7 miles of Leesburg

September 6: marched through Leesburg to within 4 miles of Potomac River

September 7: crossed Potomac at Cheek's Ford, marched to vicinity of Buckeystown

September 8: started toward Frederick, crossed Monocacy, stopped on north bank

September 9: marched toward Frederick but retraced steps; began at 5 P.M. a march toward the aqueduct of the Chesapeake and Ohio canal with orders to destroy aqueduct

September 10: in early A.M. attempted to destroy aqueduct but could not due to inadequate explosives; in P.M., marched to Point of Rocks, built bridge over canal for artillery and wagons, had crossed into Virginia by daylight

September 11: remained in camp

September 12: marched all day to vicinity of Hillsboro

September 13: passed through Hillsboro and by 10 A.M. were 5 miles from Harper's Ferry; at 6 P.M. marched to top of Loudoun Heights; marched down later in evening

September 14: at Loudoun Heights

September 15: Harper's Ferry surrenders

September 16-18: march to Sharpsburg, battle on 17th, on field the 18th, began retreat at Boteler's Ford evening of 18th

September 19: regiment passes through Shepherdstown to Winchester

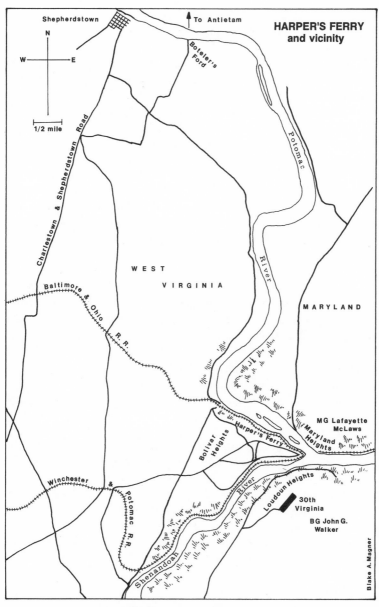

Map of Harper's Ferry

Map by Blake Magner.

49

feet below. Meanwhile, Jackson's army was in the valley behind Harper's Ferry and was surrounding General Miles and his infantry in the town.

I determined to see all that I could, so I started down to where French's Battery was firing for a better view. The Yankee howitzer shells were scraping the top of Loudoun Heights and exploding. Just as I got to French's Battery, shrapnel exploded over the battery; several men were killed and Lieutenant Robertson, a brave young officer of some eighteen to twenty years, was mortally wounded. Some of the artillerymen thought that enemy skirmishers had crossed the river and were firing on them down the side of the mountain. I thought it would be a good chance to get my command up the mountain to see everything and be in at the finish, so I hurried back to the stone wall to Captain French and General Walker. I was the first to inform them of Lieutenant Robertson's disaster. Both French and General Walker became very excited about Robertson's mortal wound and much to my surprise and disgust, Captain French refused to leave the stone wall. I thought this would be a good time to tell General Walker about the rumor of enemy skirmishers and that the artillerymen wanted my company to deploy around the battery for support. In the excitement, General Walker agreed, so I hurried back the mile and a half to my company. I reported to Colonel Harrison that I was ordered by General Walker to bring my company up and deploy them in front of the battery. The colonel did not seem to like that idea much, but as the general had ordered the move, he had to agree. I formed my company and started up the mountain in great glee, but the men did not seem very much enthused. As we got to the top of the mountain near the stone wall, a shell came over and exploded near our company. It seemed to be full of minie balls, as it broke into numerous small pieces. The men were protected behind a ledge of rocks, so I thought I would reconnoiter. I went over to the stone wall and reported to General Walker, who seemed to have forgotten that he had ordered my company to the top of the mountain. He said to hold the men in readiness until further orders.

I was anxious to get a good look, so I pushed on down the mountain to see what I could see. After going three or four hundred yards, I met a cavalryman who said that Miles had raised

Loudoun Heights

Photograph courtesy of Library of Congress.

the white flag.[6] There was a lull in the fighting about this time, so then I thought I would like to be the first Confederate in Harper's Ferry. I got down the mountain as quickly as I could and at the foot of the mountain I ran across a dismounted cavalryman, a young fellow from Orange County named Powell. He, too, was a sightseer, so I proposed that we go on down to the town. We got down to the river road, which ran above the Shenandoah about two hundred feet. We reached the ferry, and on the edge of town and across the river about one hundred yards we could see a body of Yankee troops. We were not sure if they would fire or not, but seeing a flatboat on the other side of the river, I yelled for them to bring it over. Three or four Yanks brought the boat over, and we got in. At first, we were not sure who the prisoners were. I asked them if they had surrendered, but they wouldn't say. The firing had ceased, so I put up a bold front and ordered them to row us across the river.

As soon as we were across the river, we started up to the town. After a little distance, we came across a company of Yanks in new uniforms parading along the side of the street. Their captain was making a speech in which he told them that the fortunes of war were against them this time but that they would get back to fight the rebels again. I noticed that they were a fine-looking body of men and seemed full of fight.[7] Powell and I went on in to town and found that we were the first Confederates. Some of the Yanks would say, "Here come the damn rebels."

I thought I might raise something for our commissary, so I started in a store but was met at the door by a pretty girl who slammed the door in my face, saying she wanted no rebels there. I went into the next store and ordered the proprietor to wrap up twenty pounds of coffee and ten pounds of sugar. I asked the price and it seemed low, but it was the price in greenbacks. I paid the bill in Confederate money; the merchant was chagrined but dared not refuse. Then I remembered I couldn't carry all of that coffee and sugar, so Powell and I started down the street, determined to get fine horses with accoutrements. Soon we saw some horses tied in front of a large building, which was a hospital. We walked up, picked out two horses, and began to untie them. Two or three Yankee surgeons came out and said the horses were private property and must not be molested. As we had no backing, we went on a little further into town.

I went into another store and saw a fine saber on one of the shelves. I told the merchant to pass over the saber, that I would take charge of it. He said the Quartermaster Department was nearby and had a lot of horses, so I pulled out for down there. Then I saw some Confederate cavalry down the street and felt safer. I came to a big lot filled with wagons, horses, and stores of all kinds. We walked in and found the quartermaster and his men all excited. I told him we wanted two horses apiece, the best he had. He told us to help ourselves. A lot of cavalry horses were tied to the fence, equipment and all, so we took two apiece and started out. About this time, a good many Confederate cavalry arrived, and they were all looking out to see what they could get. I was looking to see what else I could pick up when all at once a Yankee sergeant ran out from a side street and asked if I were not a Confederate officer. I said that I was, and the sergeant said, "Doubtless you have the good of the cause at heart." I replied that I did, and he said, "A lot of your men have broken into the arsenal and are helping themselves to pistols and sabers." I asked him to show me the place, so he took me down to a big building and there I found several dozen Confederate cavalrymen dismounted. They were going into the building and coming out each with new sabres and fine revolvers. One had ten or fifteen strung together and tied around a horse's neck. The Yankee sergeant said, "You see what they are doing?" I said that I did and directed the sergeant to tend my horses while I went inside. I found a lot of men inside, breaking into boxes and helping themselves to guns, pistols, and sabres. I decided that to the victor belongs the spoils, so I pitched in to help myself. I saw a box of self-cocking pistols, so I took two and stuck them in my belt.[8]

I was looking for something else to freeze to when a soldier came in and said that General Jackson was coming, so we all commenced to get away. Not wishing to see General Jackson, I hurried away as quickly as I could along with the cavalrymen. After this, I decided it would be best to get across the river as quickly as possible. Some citizens directed me to a ford down the river, but it looked too deep for anyone to cross. I asked other citizens if the river could be crossed there; some said it could, others not. About this time I heard big cheering up the street and thought that

General Jackson had arrived,[9] so I plunged in, determined to take my chances on crossing. It was terribly rough, the whole bottom strewn with boulders. Sometimes, the water was almost over the horse's back, while the next instant, I was on top of a big boulder, only to fall off again into deep water. I realized that with my plunder of pistols, overcoats, and sabers, I would be in bad shape for swimming.

After floundering and splashing, I managed to get across about two hundred yards above the Potomac. I found a road around the base of the mountain and thought it would take me to camp, but I soon found out from some citizens I was nearly eighteen miles from camp. Night was coming on and it was getting dark. After getting around the base of the mountain, I was in more open country, but I still lost the road several times, and it took nearly all night to get back to camp. I did not know where my company was but found that they had been brought back by the second lieutenant. I gave the horses to the brigade quartermaster, sold some of the plunder, and distributed the rest amongst the boys.

Just before sunup orders came for a forced march to Harper's Ferry to join Jackson, so I had to start off tired after losing a night's sleep, but I could tell the boys of my big experiences. I guess that if it had been a quiet time, I would have been put under arrest, but I was saved by the excitement and all that was going on. When we got near Harper's Ferry, our orders were to move on across the river as rapidly as possible to meet a big battle. We marched posthaste for Sharpsburg.

CHAPTER IX

Two Red Shirts at Antietam

We crossed the Potomac at Shepherdstown, where the water was swift and deep. One man drowned, and several were swept off their feet. We went into camp about dark. Lee had formed a line of battle, and we were ordered to move by light the next morning to take our positions.[1] The next morning, we ate our breakfast of hardtack and meat and got ready for the fight. Near us was the King George Company, and I saw Captain Foster of that company. He had a new pair of boots, and in putting them on, remarked that he believed he would be killed in those redtop boots. I had not put on my boots, so I determined to put on the right boot first for luck and ever since I have adhered to that.

Orders came to take position posthaste on the right of the line. After a hurried march of about two miles, we were halted to await orders. We were then near the extreme right of the line.[2] In about a half an hour, a courier brought orders to double quick to the left to support Jackson, who was being driven back. We started out and must have double quicked about two miles.[3] When we got up to where Jackson was fighting, we were ordered to throw off our knapsacks and load our guns ready for a charge. One man from each company was left to guard our baggage. I had a new uniform coat and thought it looked conspicuous, so I took it off and left it in charge of the man guarding the luggage. I never even thought that my blood red hunting shirt was even more conspicuous. We loaded our guns and were waiting when Lieutenant Saunders of the King George Company walked up to me. He had on a red shirt and said, "Rawlings, we are quite conspicuous in our red shirts." I noticed for the first time that my shirt was red. Saunders was killed in less than half an hour.

We formed a line of battle with the brigade and moved forward.[4] We began to pass over ground that had already been fought over with guns and dead and wounded in all stages of mutilation. We kept on through a cornfield and then began to get under fire. The bullets made a terrible noise as they hit the corn. We kept on through the corn and passed the Dunkard Church,

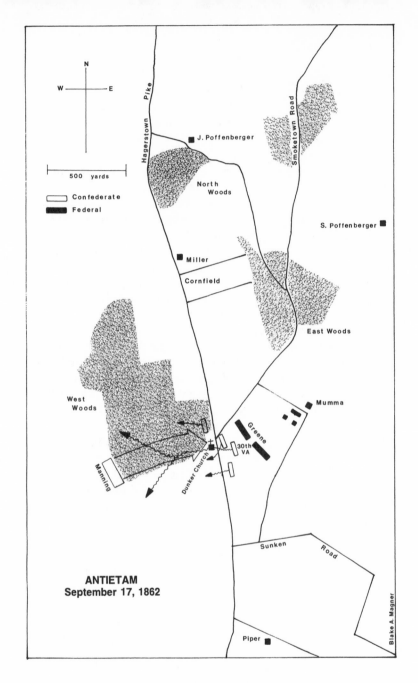

Sharpsburg, Maryland
September 17, 1862

Map by Blake Magner.

where we were ordered to charge double quick. On a hill about two or three hundred yards away was a skirmish line. They were firing at us very briskly, and as each man brought up his gun to fire, I thought he was firing at my red shirt, and I did not feel easy.[5]

We charged on the double quick over fences, keeping our line as well as we could. As we got within sixty or seventy yards of the top of the hill, the enemy line that had been lying down raised up and fired point blank at us. We heard afterwards that there were three lines of battle on the crest of the hill. We had no supports and were ordered to lie down and fire. In fact, the supports refused to come up.[6] In addition to the heavy infantry fire, a battery began playing on our regiment about this time. Four or five Napoleons were brought up on the right flank and enfiladed our line with grape and canister. Our colonel gave orders to retreat to prevent all of us from being killed. We commenced to retreat in good order, but the fire was so terrible that every man broke and got out as fast as possible. I could see a part of a rail fence about thirty yards ahead and was making good time toward it, humped up to expose no more of my body than necessary. I picked out a place on the top rail to spring over, but in this place about twenty bullets had struck the rail. There were splinters every three millimeters or more. I thought that if I went over there, the enemy would get me on the wing, so I moved a little to the right, where there was a break in the fence and men were crowding through. Here I was struck above the right eye but whether from a bullet or the barrel of a gun by one of my own men I never knew. We got through the fence, across the cornfield and past the Dunkard Church. We halted and tried to form a new line as soon as we were out of musketry fire, though the shells still came pretty lively. The Yanks did not follow. Some fresh troops came in and filled the gap while we were forming. After our column formed, we began to get some idea of our fearful loss. We went in with nearly three hundred muskets; seventy was all that we could get together on reforming. We were ordered into position further on to the right to support some other troops.[7]

In a few hours we sent over a detail to gather up the wounded and found Lieutenant Saunders of the red shirt lying at the foot of a tree near the Dunkard Church with a daguerreotype

Dunkard Church

Photograph courtesy of Library of Congress.

of his sweetheart in his hand and shot through the breast dead. In the line of battle where we had fought we found dead men stacked up in piles. Captain Foster of the new redtop boots was found dead, with one of the lieutenants lying dead on top of him. I lost eight men killed in my company at the time and more than twice that many badly wounded. Amongst the wounded was Joe Haislip. His face was black and bruised, and he said a shell had exploded in front of his face and knocked him down. I sent him back to a hospital in the rear. Thirty years later, I saw that same man, and he was telling of how he played me then. He said the firing got so hot that he decided he could not stand it any longer, and he fell down and to keep out of trouble, broke a cartridge, wet the powder, and rubbed it over his face and made up the yarn about the exploding shell. He was laughing about fooling Lieutenant Rawlings, then in command of the company.

We lay in line of battle all that day. As I was always anxious to see what was going on, I started out with Lieutenant Knox up to where the firing was. All along were many wounded fellows and one poor boy I'll never forget. He was lying at the foot of a tree with many dead men around him; he had two bullet holes, one on each side, right through the lower part of the bowels. After passing him, the bullets got to be so thick that we decided to go back to our command. We laid on our arms that night and stayed in line of battle all the next day, waiting for McClellan to attack. We gathered up our wounded to take them across the river. We began crossing the night of the next day, but I was among the rear guard and did not cross until after sunup the next morning. I ran across many wounded while on retreat and took them up to the river, where there were flatboats carrying them across. While waiting for the wounded to get on the boats, a cavalry officer came up, swearing at us to cross the river, that the Yanks were coming and that we would be captured. He ordered us very peremptorily to go down and cross. I told him I did not intend to go until my wounded were aboard. So I stayed and then went down and found my command.

We crossed the Potomac with stragglers, wagons, cavalry, and ambulances. We had hardly gotten to the other bank when the Yanks ran up guns and began firing shells at us from across the river. The Yanks had followed us up pretty close, but we kept on through Shepherdstown. The Yanks thought they had us on the

Boteler's Ford

Photograph courtesy of Library of Congress.

run, and a brigade or two of them crossed over the river after us. The Confederate rear guard then formed and charged and drove them back in the river, killing a good many. Others drowned. So they were content with their own side after that.

The ladies of Shepherdstown were out in the street with buckets of coffee and biscuits that they would hand the troops as they passed along. They also dressed the wounds of those able to walk. One man in my company was shot in the hand, and a lot of girls dressed his wound. He said it made him feel good to have those girls dressing his wound. It reminded him of a snowbird hopping over an ash bank. We went into camp and waited for the Yanks to cross, but they did not. We began to go out foraging in the countryside. At one large farmhouse we were well-treated with plenty to eat -- apple butter and wasp's nest bread, or salt rising bread, as they called it. At this house lived two lively, red-headed girls. We got so well acquainted that we boys got to hugging and kissing the girls. One day the old grandfather came into the room and caught me with my arm around one of the girls. I withdrew it very quickly at the old man's entrance, but he saw me and said he wanted it understood that those girls had a Kentucky farm apiece and were not to be trifled with. We all made up that we would try to get a lock of the girls' hair and would claim the privilege of cutting if off ourselves. We all got a lock, and about the last we saw of those girls their heads looked like a crow's nest.

From a Fredericksburg Newspaper After the Battle of Antietam

THE THIRTIETH VIRGINIA REGIMENT

This noble regiment -- which has covered itself with a glory that shall never pale -- is without blankets, clothing and shoes. They ask their fathers, brothers, sisters, wives and friends, in this the section of their nativity or adoption, to take measures to relieve their necessities. Thank God, we need not to stir up the people of

Fredericksburg and the surrounding country by any long drawn or ardent appeal in their behalf. The soldiers' necessity is our necessity; their want, our want. The heart that cannot feel, and will not promptly respond, must be encrusted in an iceberg of selfishness, and for one we would not receive an offering from any such. With very rare exceptions indeed there is not a family in town that cannot furnish at least one blanket; and we suppose there is not a matron in Caroline, Spotsylvania, Stafford and King George but will respond. Bring out the woolen goods from your home looms, and if need be, divide what you have with the brave and gallant, whose comrades have already sealed their devotion to their county with their life's blood.

Let Capt. Alexander receive a warm greeting and assist him with a lavish hand so that the hearts of our brave boys may have tangible evidence that though absent they are dearer than ever to the hearts of those at home.

The following communication from the Commanding Officer of the Brigade we append:

ARMY OF NORTHERN VIRGINIA
Martinsburg, Sept. 24th, 1862

In the long and fatiguing marches and brilliant engagements with the enemy, which, by the help of God, have resulted in driving the enemy from Virginia, the 30th Virginia and 3rd Arkansas Volunteers, battling side by side, have borne a distinguished part, and now at the approach of cool weather, they find themselves destitute of shoes and blankets.

Our government being without the means of supplying their wants in time to prevent much suffering to those gallant men, I have no hesitation in appealing to the patriotic citizens of

Fredericksburg and surrounding country for such contributions of blankets and clothing as their pressing wants demand. Capt. R. H. Alexander is authorized to receive and transmit such articles as may be contributed.

J. G. WALKER
Brig. Gen. C.S.A.

CHAPTER X

The Paper Collar Incident

We camped near Culpeper[1] for a while in the fall but then marched down to Fredericksburg and found the Yanks on the heights on the north side of the Rappahannock. Our friends from Caroline and Spotsylvania came out to see us. There was an old fellow on horseback with his saddle bags full of apples. He had some relatives in the Caroline County regiment and ran across them on the march. Some of the boys went up to speak to him and would say, "How are you, Uncle Bob?" He would run his hands in his saddle pockets and would give them an apple. He seemed to have a lot of nephews. Some of the men in my company ran up also, and he spoke to them, giving them apples, and shaking hands all around until the apples were gone. He said he never knew he had so many nephews in the Thirtieth Virginia. When the apples gave out, Uncle Bob was not as popular.

We went into camp on Telegraph Road, a few miles in the rear of town and awaited developments.[2] In a short while, the Yanks threw pontoon bridges[3] across the river near the falls and commenced crossing over. A day or two before, all citizens had been ordered out of Fredericksburg, and they all came marching out -- men, women, children, dogs -- everything. They took up quarters in the Salem Baptist Church three or four miles out of town and anywhere else they could.[4]

Our company was ordered to take position in about the center of the line not far from the Barnard House.[5] The enemy gradually crossed the river and advanced against Barksdale's Mississippians, who fought for every foot of ground and killed lots of Yanks while slowly retreating to the foot of Marye's Heights. All day and all night the Yanks crossed on the pontoon bridges. One was placed at about the present location of the wharf. Our line extended from Hamilton's Crossing, held by Jackson, three or four miles to the foot of Marye's Heights. From my position in the line of battle, I had a splendid view of the country to the right. I could see the whole of the Barnard farm and the Yanks' line of battle next to the river. Early one morning, the enemy began to advance and

64

attacked Jackson on the left. As their line of battle started moving up, they started a red fox, and he ran for the Confederate line and then started back to the Yanks. He ran back and forth with both armies yelling at him. Our part of the line was never attacked. It was in this battle that the gallant old soldier, Maxcy Gregg, was killed. Later in the day came a rumor that General Jackson had proposed attacking with the bayonet and driving the enemy into the river. We were expecting a desperate fight, but the attack was never made. No doubt it would have been successful.

A few nights later, the Yanks withdrew across the river. They seemed satisfied after that battle, and we went into winter quarters down near Guiney's Station, near Vauxhall, the home of Uncle John Holladay. My relatives came to see me and I got permission to spend the night at Vauxhall now and then. On one occasion, Ma came to Vauxhall, and I got permission to be absent for one night. I brushed up and tried to look my best. I managed to get a paper collar from somewhere. On the road to Vauxhall, I passed through different brigades of the division and tried to keep out of sight so the men would not poke fun at me. But the men began to notice I was a stranger, and one would say, "Come out of that collar, I know you are thar."[6] I did not enjoy it, so I circled around to try to avoid the camp, but I soon ran into another one. These boys said, "Come out of that collar. I can see your heels sticking out." I was much relieved to get to Vauxhall.

CHAPTER XI

The Great Snowball Battle

Here occurred the biggest snowball battle[1] of my experience. We had about five or six inches of good snow one night. The next morning was clear, and snowballs began to fly before breakfast. I heard great cheering and the Confederate yell coming down the lines. I did not know what it was at first. As it came nearer, it got louder and louder, with thousands yelling and shouting. We all gathered together, guessing what the row was. At last in an open field about three hundred yards away we saw a line of battle extending a mile or more. There were no guns, only shouting. Officers on horseback charged over the regiment camped on the field, and we could see what looked like a snowstorm accompanying them. About this time, a courier came galloping in to camp, swinging his hat, and saying that a certain command had formed a line of battle and was charging everything and for us to get in line of battle and manufacture snowballs. The boys formed a line of battle, and some of the officers assumed their commands. We sent out a skirmish line about one hundred yards in front; the skirmishers had their hats and arms full of snowballs, but the skirmish line was soon driven and captured. On they came, yelling and shouting, very like a Yankee charge, and it felt like a battle. I could see the whole air filled with flying snowballs, like a snowstorm. Our line held our ground at first, but we were skittish because we were outnumbered five to one. When they saw our line of battle, they got noisier still and sent out a flanking movement. When they got close, we opened with snowballs, but we could not hold them, and our line broke. Those of us who did not retreat were in squads throwing snowballs as fast as we could. About a dozen of us were doing what we could when some of them spotted my uniform and rushed to grab me. In spite of my efforts, about five or six carried me off, yelling for me to surrender. Then my men rallied and countercharged and commenced using their fists and like to pull me apart trying to recapture me. But the numbers were too many, and my boys had to skedaddle while I was carried ignominiously to the rear. Finally, I was offered parole if I would take the oath of allegiance to the Confederacy.

The snowballers charged right over our camp, and a great many men were very incensed. We were invited to join in, and many did, so away they went to the next camp, down to other commands, overrunning and capturing them likewise. It was very exciting, and fist fighting happened right often; only not being able to get guns saved worse trouble. Our colors were captured but were returned afterwards. The regimental officers stayed close in their tents, but some of their tents were pulled down. They felt incensed and mortified.

CHAPTER XII

Promoted to Captain on the Field of Battle

We were ordered from camp in mid-winter and sent down towards Richmond. There were rumors of an advance of the enemy up the James River. Toward the end of March, our division was ordered to Suffolk, as a large force of the enemy had captured that town and were supposed to be on the road to Richmond from there. After hard marching, we stopped near the Dismal Swamp and went into camp for several weeks. Here on the edge of the swamp I had my first mess of frog legs. To be in fashion, I would eat the legs, but I was not very fond of them. Later in the Spring, we started for Suffolk on a forced march. It was hot, and the long, severe marches went hard with us. We were in a poor country with small prospects for foraging, and food was short. Finally, we arrived near Suffolk and took up our position right next to the Dismal Swamp, where we threw out pickets. The skirmishing was pretty sharp every day.[1]

I had then been commanding my company nearly twelve months, Captain Day being away sick. During the previous winter, orders from Richmond said that all officers being absent a certain length of time should report or be dropped from the rolls. As Day did not report, he was dropped, and I, as the next officer in line, was promoted. First I had to take an exam for the promotion, so while under fire and in the line of battle, I stood my examination. Major Willis of the Fifteenth Regiment and two other officers asked the questions. I had no trouble. I was asked a few questions about tactics and drill, and finally Major Willis told me that I knew as much as he did.

The country was very poor, and our fare was rough -- hardtack, fat meat, and corn meal every now and then and not enough of anything. For the past few months, I had had with me a cook, a colored boy named Joe, who was one of Pa's servants. I had not seen him for several days and did not know whether he had gone over to the Yankees or not. Finally, when we were under fire and in line of battle, Joe showed up. He accounted for his absence by saying he had been out foraging and to prove it he had an old coffee pot with a stewed chicken in it. I was pleased with the stew, so I let Joe off easy. There was a little line of breastworks near where I was talking to Joe, and as nothing much was happening, I was sitting around in the woods in the rear of the breastworks. I was sitting on the end of a pine log when I got the chicken, and I took a drink of the soup out of the spout and found it very good. About that time, Major Gouldin came along, and I thought I would divide with the major. A shell was coming over now and then, so I moved down from the end of the log and offered the major some of the soup. The major's appetite was not good under fire, so he declined with thanks. In a few minutes, a shell came very low. It passed near my head and struck in the ground a few feet in the rear. It exploded and made a big hole. Had the major taken some soup, he would have lost his head. I saved my soup, and the Major his head. Looking behind, I saw Joe behind a big pine tree near where the shell had struck, the whites of his eyes rolling.

After some days of skirmishing and slight fighting, we were suddenly ordered to retreat and took up a line of march to Petersburg along the railroad, the Yanks harassing our rear. This was about the time of the Battle of Chancellorsville,[2] which we did not hear about until we reached Petersburg. We became separated from our baggage, and I had no blanket. It was cold at night in the open air. In my sleep I rolled into the fire, which awakened me. My whole jacket front was ablaze, and half of my jacket was burned off. We soon heard the particulars of the Battle of Chancellorsville and the news of General Jackson's death from a wound received at the hands of his own men. We went into camp near Richmond and took part in the obsequies at General Jackson's death. Then we moved across the James and camped below Richmond.

CHAPTER XIII

My Division Went Into Pickett's Charge Without Me

After a few weeks, we heard rumors that Lee had commenced a second Maryland campaign. We were ordered to take position on the North Anna River near Hanover Court House. We were detailed to guard the railroad bridges in the rear of the army during the advance into Maryland and Pennsylvania. Here, with the exception of a good many alarms and Yankee cavalry, the brigade was stationed during the Gettysburg Campaign. We escaped the hardships and danger of that memorable campaign, and my division went into Pickett's charge at Gettysburg without me. After the retreat across the Potomac, we were ordered to rejoin our command, which we met some days later while passing through Winchester.[1] It was very sad to see the terrible gaps made in the ranks at the Battle of Gettysburg. When our old division passed us, I remember seeing regiments commanded by captains and brigades by colonels -- a mere skeleton of what when last seen were full brigades.

We went into camp near Orange Court House, and then our brigade was ordered to Southwestern Virginia and East Tennessee, where we were to meet Longstreet on his return from the East Tennessee campaign, which resulted in the Battle of Chickamauga.[2] We went down to East Tennessee as far as Jonesboro and then on to Zollicoffer. Here, in a raid, the cavalry surrounded Rogersville and captured a number of prisoners. About this time, the battle of Chickamauga took place. We were camped at Abingdon, and many troops passed through that place on their way East. While in camp there, we saw many stragglers from the Battle of Chickamauga, among whom was a stray cavalryman, who came in camp along the railroad one night, dressed in a splendid cavalry uniform and big top boots. He claimed he had done wonders at Chickamauga; in fact, he boasted quite a lot and was dubbed "Chickamauga." After recounting his hairbreadth escape and great prowess and after taking our hospitality, he found a place to sleep near the depot. We cautioned him to be careful, as the country was full of toughs, both with and without their commands.

The next morning, we were surprised to see a soldier sans hat, coat, or boots, and it was our old friend "Chickamauga," who had gone to sleep near the depot and had had his things stolen by the boys at night. He was very different from the gay cavalryman of the day before -- quite crestfallen -- and would hardly answer to the name of "Chickamauga."

CHAPTER XIV

Yankee Hospitality

While we were in camp near Bristol in November, I applied for and received a furlough to visit my home in Spotsylvania for two weeks. Leaving my command in East Tennessee, I journeyed to Eastern Virginia. I stopped in Petersburg and drew some gray cloth from the Quartermaster Department and ordered a uniform to be made. The cloth was two or three hundred dollars in Confederate money, which seemed cheap at the time.

I arrived in Fredericksburg a day or two afterwards and visited Clem Harris, who loaned me his gray horse to ride home, twenty miles away. I reached home the next day a little after dark and was welcomed by Ma, Pa, and my sisters, who were very much surprised by my unexpected appearance.[1]

The next morning, I ordered Henry, a young Negro, to take the horse back to Clem Harris. After he had been gone about half an hour, Henry came back full tilt, saying, "Marse Benny, the whole country down there is full of Yankees!" Very soon refugees came by our house with stock, cattle, and horses, running away from the Yanks, who were in force between my home and the Court House at Spotsylvania. (This was in late November 1863, when Meade had crossed the Rappahannock, expecting to surprise the Army of Northern Virginia. But when after severe skirmishing, he found Lee squarely in his front, ready and eager for the fray, he seems to have become suddenly convinced of the truth of the old adage, "That prudence was the better part of valor," so he hastily fell back across the river to his old camps.)

The Yankee army was said to be only four or five miles across the country and to satisfy myself of the truth, I decided to go out on a "Scout." I took my father's double-barreled shotgun and my pistol and started out across country on foot. I took a path across country that led me to White Hall, a prominent place in the neighborhood and where the Yanks were reported to be. Sure enough, in approaching cautiously the manor house, I saw a column of Yankee cavalry on the road and decided at once to ascertain their strength. I plunged into the wood and approached the road very

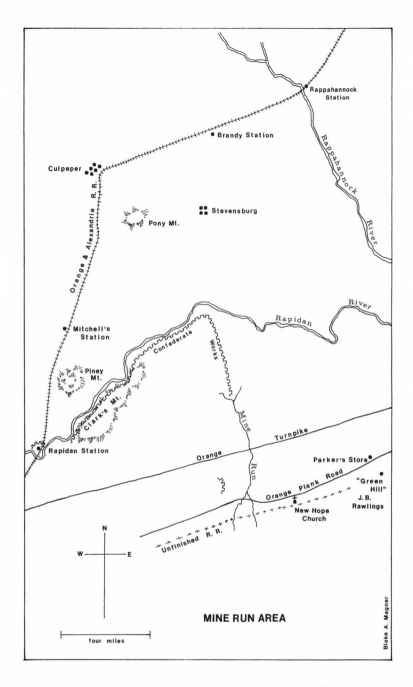

Map labels: Rappahannock Station, Brandy Station, Culpeper, Orange & Alexandria R. R., Stevensburg, Pony Mt., Rappahannock River, Mitchell's Station, Rapidan River, Confederate Works, Piney Mt., Clark's Mt., Rapidan Station, Orange Turnpike, Mine Run, Parker's Store, "Green Hill" J.B. Rawlings, Orange Plank Road, New Hope Church, Unfinished R. R.

N W E

MINE RUN AREA

four miles

Blake A. Magner

Mine Run

During the Mine Run Campaign Ben Rawlings was captured while at his home.

73

cautiously. I found the road filled with cavalry and artillery headed west in the direction of Orange Court House. Crawling as near the road as possible, I tried to estimate the pieces of artillery and number of cavalry. I found what I took to be the rear guard of Sheridan's cavalry, and they soon passed. Then, feeling confident that one or two stragglers would follow, I got directly in the road and was soon rewarded by seeing two men gallop up the road. These I halted as they came round a bend, and I then made them ride off Indian file in front of me into the woods. When some distance in, I made them dismount. After selecting the best horse, and they having already been disarmed, I made them mount together on one horse in front of me, and I streaked for home. The family was much surprised when I came riding up with the prisoners.[2] I turned them over to Hampton's Command during the day, the receipt of which I still hold.[3]

Unfortunately, I stayed at home that night, and during the night the house was surrounded by a regiment of Yankee cavalry, and I was captured.[4] In company with some one hundred or more unfortunate comrades, under a strong and vigilant guard, we were taken to the rear, preceding by some hours the main army. It was during this retreat that we saw the notorious Dr. Mary Walker,[5] the first and I suppose the only female doctor or surgeon in the war. She was riding a cavalry saddle with a foot in each stirrup, seemingly very much at home. She had on a certain kind of bloomer costume, and the prisoners looked on her in great amazement. She is still living and is as mannish as ever.

After some days we were loaded in box cars and under a heavy guard were sent to Washington and consigned to the Old Carroll Prison, sometimes known as the Old Capitol Prison.[6] Here we found a thousand or more other prisoners who welcomed us boisterously by yelling at the top of their lungs, "Fresh fish! Fresh fish!" We were then separated from our private soldiers, the officers in the upper floors and the privates in the lower stories. We found the commandant to be the celebrated Capt. Woods, a very rough, profane man but kindhearted. He was an old chum of Col. Ould, our Commissioner for Exchange of Prisoners. Our fare at this prison was very good and plenty of it. Belle Boyd,[7] the famous Confederate spy, was incarcerated in this prison but was exchanged a few days before we arrived. There was also Capt.

Dr. Mary Edwards Walker

Photograph courtesy of Library of Congress.

75

Old Capitol Prison in Washington, D.C.

Photograph courtesy of Massachusetts Commandery Military Order of the Loyal Legion and the USAMHI.

76

Cleggett Fitzhugh,[8] who, in the John Brown Raid, captured Cook, a lieutenant of John Brown's. Also there was Julian Lee,[9] a member of the famous Lee family and as gallant a little fellow as ever lived.

On one of the front windows were the stains from the life blood of the gallant Lt. Sherrard, who after paying one of the guards a large sum to let him escape through the window, was shot through and through by the same sentinel who treacherously lured him to his death. Sherrard was shot through the bowels and suffered horribly before relieved by death. The treacherous soldier soon fell sick himself and died in great agony. Many thought Capt. Woods had him poisoned, as Sherrard was a friend of Woods and no one regretted the incident more than Woods.

Captain Fitzhugh used to tell a very amusing anecdote of Sherrard and a Dutch Yankee Major. It seemed that Sherrard occupied a room alone and that this Yankee Major was sent in from the front for stealing. He was a very large, fine-looking German with a showy cavalry uniform. Capt. Woods hardly knew what to do with him but finally decided to put him in the room with Sherrard for a while. The guard put him in the room and shut the door. The Major looked scornfully at Sherrard and at last asked the question, "Who the Hell be you?" Sherrard, restraining his anger, replied, "I am a Confederate officer and a prisoner of war." "The Hell you be," said the Major. "I'll see that Capt. Woods is court-martialed for putting a Union officer in the room with a damn rebel! Corporal of the guard, corporal of the guard!" he shouted with all his might. Upon the arrival of the corporal, he demanded to see Capt. Woods at once. Upon the appearance of Woods, he cursed and swore outrageously, "You damn rascal, you put me -- a U.S. officer -- in the room with a damn rebel. I'll court-martial you and cashier you -- you damn villain." After listening to this abuse for a while, Woods turned to Sherrard and said, "Lt. Sherrard, can't you tame this Dutch whelp? I leave him in your charge," and he left the room. This was ducks for Sherrard, who was not near as large as the Dutchman but of fair size and built like a gladiator. Stepping out in the middle of the floor, he said very firmly, "Come, dry up -- I've had enough of that." This seemed to enrage the major still further and he commenced to fight. Neither was armed but with what nature gave them. Sherrard seized the major around the body and then commenced a real tug of war, but it did not last long, for soon the

Dutchman lay flat on his back blowing like a porpoise. Sherrard, as fresh as a daisy, was on his feet, and seizing the Dutchman by the foot, he placed his own foot on his crotch and with a dexterous twist pulled off his great heavy cavalry boot with spur attached and brandished it over his head, saying quietly, "Look here, you Dutch hound, you do as I order you or I will knock your brains out in two minutes. Now, not a word without my permission. I desire you to take the oath to the Southern Confederacy. You repeat it after me word for word. Do you understand?" Not receiving an answer, Sherrard gave him a good kick in his exposed anatomy. The Dutchman began to plead most piteously. "Shut up and do as I bid you," said Sherrard, who then made him repeat the long oath word for word. After getting through, he was made to apologize for his conduct and was told to lie in the same position until Capt. Woods came around, which was seven hours later. Capt. Woods rejoiced. "I'll take him out tomorrow, Sherrard, and if he gets unruly again, I will send him back to you for another dose." He did not return.

Excuse this digression; I only speak of this as an actual occurrence and to show you that the Johnny Rebs were ever ready for fun and frolic. Our stay at the Old Capitol prison was for nearly two months, and then we were ordered to pack up to leave at a few minute's notice. This we much regretted, for we were sure we would be worsted in the change. We were taken directly to Fort McHenry[10] on Baltimore Harbor. This was, as we had anticipated, not for the better. Although we got enough to eat, it was dished out to us like so many pigs. A big Irishman would go through the barracks with two large camp kettles with the beef cut up in small pieces, which he would pick up with his naked hands and toss it to each one of the prisoners. Another man would come along with crackers and coffee. Each prisoner had his own tin cup, which was filled, and so many crackers were counted out for him.[11]

Ben Rawlings' Receipt for the Two Federal Prisoners

Recd Orange Spotsyvani [sic] Va. Nov 27 '63 of
Capt. B.C. Rawlings, Co. D, 30th Va. Regt. Inft.
one Horse   one saddle   one Bridle   one halter
captured property   also 2 federal prisoners

> R. C. Shirer Lt.
> Cmd Scouts
> Hampton's Div

Note Informing Family That Ben Rawlings was a Prisoner of War

Mrs. Woolfry,[12]

You will please inform my family that I
am a Prisoner of War, and Capt. Benj. Rawlings
also, we are on our way to Washington City this
the 28th November 1863.

> W. D. Foster
> Capt. Benj. C. Rawlings

*This note was wrapped around a rock and thrown
into the yard of friends as prisoners were marched by.*

Sentence in italics added later by family member.

Note Wrapped Around Rock

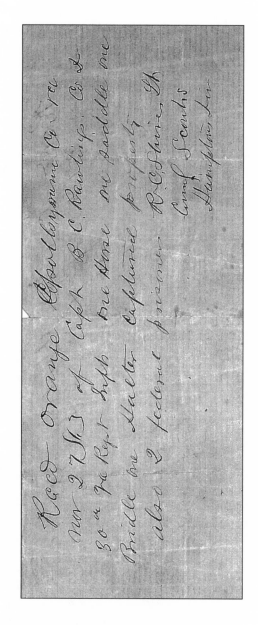

Recd Orange C.H. Va
Nov 27th 1863 at Capt B.C. Rawlings, Co L
30th Va Regt Inft one Horse one Saddle one
Bridle one Halter captured property
also 2 federal prisoners R.C.Shire, Lt
Comd Scouts
Hampton Leg

Receipt for Prisoners

From Lt. John Rawlings to Ann Rawlings, Ben's Mother

Camp Near Tenn. Jan 24 1864

Dear Cousin Ann,[13]

Your letter informing me of Ben's capture came to hand a few days ago. I should have written sooner in reply but have been prevented by constant marching. I am truly sorry for him and hope he may receive kind treatment from the enemy. I can well understand how much you are all grieved and be assured that you have my most sincere sympathy in this unexpected trouble. We all miss him very much and hope he may soon be exchanged although there seems but little prospect at present. Your request with regard to his interests will be attended to as far as within me lies. You mention some leather for a pair of boots he expected to get. He left the money with one of the men to buy it but he failed to get it from the Tanner and still holds the money. There is some money due him in the Regt. which I will secure for him. I do not know the amount for all the parties are not now here but will be here before very long. His overcoat I have and will take care of until I have a safe opportunity to send it to you. There is nothing else here except one or two blankets which I will take care of. Whether he left anything at Petersburg when he came out here or not I do not know. I was at home at the time. I suppose if he did leave anything he took it home with him when he went home. We are expecting to return to Virginia very soon, when I will write more fully about his money matters. So far I have been able to do nothing on account of no one having any money, the men not having been paid since last fall. Lieut. Beazley requests that if you will send his carpet sack which he lent Ben by a messenger

Lieut. Humphries[14] will send to your house. There is also a sash belonging to Lieut. H. also a box of pins and a set of military buttons which he wishes you to send. These things are in Ben's clothes chest. Lieut. Humphries will take this letter to Va. He is going on furlough. With best wishes for yourself and family I remain yours truly.

J. L. Rawlings

CHAPTER XV

I Starve at Point Lookout

We remained at McHenry for one month, when we were suddenly ordered to pack up without knowing our destination. We feared the change would be for the worse, and in this we were not mistaken. We were put on a side-wheel steamer and taken down the bay to Point Lookout. This place was admirably suited for a prison camp, being a narrow strip of land lying between the Potomac and Chesapeake Bay. The stockade was placed across the peninsula, extending from shore to shore. We were quartered in large Sibley tents,[1] in the center of which we could have a small fire. The wood furnished was insufficient to keep us warm in cold weather, and the rations, whilst not abundant, were sufficient to keep us from suffering. Our rations were ever so much better than those given to the privates in the next pen, who died like flies from insufficient rations, clothing, and bedding. They had an almost total lack of firewood in the coldest weather.[2]

The prisoners were confined in yards several acres in extent, fenced in by a board fence about eighteen feet high with a broad shelf about three feet from the top, on which were placed the sentinels. There was what was called a dead line, ten feet from the fence on the inside, where, if the prisoners crossed, they were shot down without mercy. One day in spreading out my blanket to sun, I inadvertently got near the dead line, and but for a comrade who yelled a timely warning, I would have been shot down without knowing my peril.

Here was our first experience with colored troops, who constituted about a third of the garrison. There were several instances where former masters recognized their quondam slaves in the sentinels posted on the parapet of the pen enclosing our quarters. These Negroes were very insolent and some days would shoot down prisoners who got too near the dead line. "Bottom rail on top now" was their favorite expression when speaking of the changed relations to their former masters. Sometimes we were reminded of our peril by the forcible remark, "White man, ball in this gun for smoking to get at you. Do as I say, white man."

Notwithstanding the difficulty of escape from the fort, many of our boys attempted it; a few succeeded in getting away, but most were soon recaptured and severely punished. I myself escaped but was recaptured in forty-eight hours and put in a dark cell for two weeks.

It was during my term of imprisonment at Pt. Lookout that I witnessed the most gallant action that I ever saw during the whole four years of the war, and I saw the white flag at Sumter and Appomattox. I was sitting in our tent one afternoon, whiling away the tedious hours, playing euchre with my messmates, when we were startled by angry and excited voices interspersed with fearful oaths. Hastily crawling to the door of the tent, a most bloodcurdling scene presented itself. A squad of Negro soldiers with fixed bayonets and cocked muskets swept past our door, yelling and cursing like madmen. The first impression was that the Negro regiment had broken through all restraint and were bent upon a wholesale massacre, but a moment later we could distinguish their threats to be directed towards a certain party. Cries of "Let me see him and I will blow him to Hell;" "Show me the damned Rebel and I'll cut his heart out." With these savage yells and curses at a double quick step they stopped before a certain tent some twenty yards above us and on the opposite side of the street, and with drawn bayonet and cocked guns, seemed to be on the brink of rushing in. The officer of the guard rushed up and ordered the infuriated Negroes back to the guardhouse. They returned slowly and sullenly with many a dire threat. The din kept up some time, and we thought the whole camp would be massacred and began to cast about us for stones and sticks to defend ourselves.

Afterwards, the lieutenant came back with a Negro guard and arrested a young man in the tent, and we sadly saw him go, as we thought, to certain death. The trouble, we soon ascertained, was this. The young man was returning from the cookhouse, when the Negro guard called to him in a threatening tone and language, something about his business in the cookhouse. The young man made some reply and excuse, but kept on his way to his tent. The Negro swore he sassed him and called frantically for the other guards, who ran to the young man's tent. At this point, a single Confederate officer, fierce and determined-looking, bounded out of the tent with quick and tiger-like springs before the Negroes, who seemed to hesitate a moment, could enter the tent. This small, delicate-looking officer sprang before them and in a commanding tone ordered them back. He seemed to be unarmed, but there were death and fury in his eye, and it overcame the brutal Negroes. They fell back a pace but continued their fearful threats and curses. With not another word but with form erect and flashing eyes he stood proudly in the door of the tent. The Lord only knows what might have been the result, for the long roll was frantically beating, and the Negroes' regiment was rushing to the scene.

After the excitement had subsided, we crowded around the Gallant Louisianian and inquired what he proposed to have done. He quietly remarked that he had a Bowie knife up his sleeve and if the black devils had entered the tent, he would have disemboweled several of them before being killed himself. I know not whether he is living or dead, but I take off my hat to him as the most gallant man I ever saw.

After several months at Point Lookout, we were suddenly shipped up the coast to Fort Delaware,[3] crowded almost to suffocation in the hold of a navy vessel. This place we found to be the worst in our experience. We were both starved and maltreated generally. The long summer days seemed interminable.

We were fed but twice a day. In the morning about nine, we had what was termed breakfast, consisting of a cup of colored water called coffee, two crackers, and a piece of bacon about the size of a silver dollar. We got our dinner about three o'clock, and in place of what they called coffee, we got a small cup of very weak and poor bean soup; sometimes we found a bean but very rarely. The rest of our dinner consisted of a small cube of fat bacon, two crackers, or a piece of baker's bread. A hungry man could have eaten the rations of four men and not felt satisfied. This would have to suffice about eighteen hours until breakfast. My continuous and persistent appetite over the years I've attributed to being half-starved for so long. There is no question the government allotted full rations but allowed the prison authorities to steal it from the defenseless prisoners. It was a common report of the amount of sugar, coffee, and bacon the authorities sold each month. A great deal has been said about Andersonville, and I have no doubt there was a great deal of suffering there, but at that same time our own army in the field was fighting and marching on short rations. We shared with our prisoners what we had ourselves.

Remember that a great government with unlimited resources starved prisoners that they refused to exchange. It is enough to bring a blush of shame to the cheek of any honest supporter of "the best government the world ever saw."[4] "O, Liberty, what atrocities are perpetrated in thy name."

After some time a lot of the prisoners were drafted to be sent to Charleston to be put under our own fire in retaliation for some act of the Confederate government which I have now forgotten. A little while after that, a certain percent of the prisoners who were thought to be in a dying condition were selected for exchange. At that time, I was in a most emaciated condition and had reached a state of mind perfectly indifferent to the future so much that I did not care to offer myself as a possibility for exchange. Some of the older men insisted that I be sent before the board, which much to my surprise, passed me at once.[5] We were then taken down to Fort Monroe by the steamer *New York* and from there up the James River by a boat of our own. While on board the *New York*, we had plenty to eat, and they made coffee in a most peculiar way. They would place two large forty or fifty gallon casks on the deck and then pour in a three gallon bucket of ground coffee and then a bucket of sugar and then fill the barrels with water. They took a rubber hose, put one end in the barrel and connected the other with the steam chest of the boat engine, which would have the whole thing boiling in two minutes.

After we were transferred to our own boats, we soon reached Richmond under our own colors.[6] There we had a jolly time greeting friends, were paid off and given indefinite furloughs home. There with kind friends and relatives, good fare, and plenty of good old apple jack, in two months I was ready to report to the trenches around Richmond. So ended my experience in Yankee prisons. That I escaped with my life can only be ascribed to a kind providence that has always taken care of me through all the dangers of an eventful and adventurous life and will, I trust, be ever merciful and kind to the end, which cannot be far off to this broken and decrepit old soldier.

The Steamer *New York*

Photograph courtesy of Library of Congress.

From Ben Rawlings to His Father While Imprisoned at Point Lookout

Point Lookout MD Feb. 26th 64
Mr. James B. Rawlings

Dear Father,

Hoping that this may reach you. I write a few lines to inform you of my whereabouts. Have not heard from you or any of the family since my capture. Wrote some months since. Am doing as well as can be expected. Hope you all are well and in good spirits. When you write write only one page of note paper. Only family matters. Unsealed. Care of Comm. Ould. Pt. Lookout Hammond Hospital. Ward 15. Not sick. Quarters for officers. W. Foster is well. Send me by flag of truce, 20 lbs. chewing tobacco. Write to a friend to deliver to Comm. Ould with my address. Also, send me some greenback's.[7] Jas. Powell at Carroll Prison, Wash. D.C. well, love to all, write soon.

Yours,

B.C. Rawlings, Capt., Co. D 30th Va. Inf.
Prisoner of War
Pt. Lookout Maryland. Send me address of Wm. Harris

Letter from Ben Rawlings to His Mother While Imprisoned at Point Lookout

Point Lookout March 1st 1864
Mrs. Jas. B. Rawlings

My Dear Mother,

A large number of officers are expected to leave for Dixie and Parole. Capt. Lee very kindly offers to visit you to inform you as regards myself. Wrote a few days ago by Flag of Truce. If I am not exchanged soon send me greenbacks by first opportunity. Have them delivered to Comm. Ould. Also 20 lbs chewing tobacco. Send certificate for receipt for the horses and prisoners to Lt. Humphries. No, you may keep it for myself. Jas. Powell is at the Old Carroll Prison, Wash. D.C. and well when I heard from him. W. Foster is well, & Dr. Smith also. You should be careful not to allow yourselves to become in contact with the Yankee army on its next advance. Save what you can. Fall back with the negroes. No more at present, doing well, only regret being idle. Extend to Capt. Lee the utmost hospitality. He is a generous officer. Hoping you all will not suffer in the next campaign. I remain with love to all.

Your devoted son,

Benjamin C. Rawlings
address me as prisoner of war
Pt. Lookout Hammond Hos. Ward. 15

Letter to Ann Rawlings from S. W. Allen, Minister, Former
Prisoner at Point Lookout

Applewood, May 10 1864
Mrs. J. B. Rawlings,

My dear sister,

Yours of the 9th was received yesterday
and it gives me pleasure to give you all the
information I have concerning your son. When I
arrived at Pt. Lookout from Johnson's Island in
Feb. I found him there. He was in the Gen.
Hospital and we were placed in the same building.
I saw him every day -- eating at the same table
together. About the 10th of March he, with all of
the *well* officers, was sent out to the officers camp,
which was a large plank pen of about 31 acres, and
was placed in tents. I never saw him after he went
there, though some came inside the hospital limits
every day. They all said they were pretty
comfortable. Two days they were guarded by
negro soldiers -- one day by white. To the Officers,
the negroes were polite and respectful, but very
oppressive to the privates who were in another
large pen -- but no intercourse between the
officers and privates was allowed. Capt. Rawlings
was generally well -- and had been supplied with
new clothes. There were ladies in Baltimore who
furnished every Confederate officer with a nice
suit. I did not hear him speak of getting money
from home, but I know many did. The Provost
Marshal told me, he got over 100 packages from
the South in one flag of truce boat. It is much
better to have money, for then we could buy fruit
and cheese and such things to eat. A great many
never had a cent, and appeared to get along pretty
well. He can do much better *with* money but he
didn't suffer as much as you might imagine without

it. The prisoners need papers, tobacco, and letters. I saw only one southern paper while in prison the "Sentinel" of the 5th March. It is just as easy to send things to a prisoner *from* Richmond as it is for the Yankees to send these things *to* Richmond for theirs and yet it is seldom done.

There are many ways in which prisoners spend their time and according to their tastes, they can be profitably employed or not as they choose. Imprisonment is a great evil and one suffers more in mind than in body -- but like all other human ills -- there are mitigations even in prison life. I therefore think your son will make himself comfortable and as Pt. Lookout is a very healthy place, I do not think you need fear greatly for his health. All are praying and hoping for release, but I am sorry to say, I see but little hope for it. There are still nearly 3,000 officers and over 20,000 privates in prison, not including those taken during the present campaign, and some of them have been imprisoned 10 months and upward. Hundreds and I may say thousands have died and hundreds have taken the oath of allegiance to escape the horrible sufferings of prison life.

I am much obliged to you for your kind sympathy -- when stationed in King & Q. I saw your daughter often -- kindly remember me to her. If I can give information upon any particular point which I have not done in this hasty letter I will do so with much pleasure. We are all in anxiety here. The two armies are only 12 miles above us and we hear them fighting every day. I was at the battlefield below Richmond on Monday last. Many of my neighbors were dreadfully wounded and some killed -- two I had baptized.

With very great respect
Your friend   S. W. Allen

From the Richmond *Enquirer* Friday, September 2, 1864
Page 2, Column 1

Capt. B. C. Rawlings, Company D, 30th Virginia regiment, was taken prisoner near Chancellorsville the last of November, 1863. Last heard from at Point Lookout.

Any information concerning him will be thankfully received by his father or brother, at Hadensville, Goochland County, Va.

Z. H. Rawlings

Northern papers please copy

Letter to Ann Rawlings from Lt. P. L. W. Thornton,
Former Prisoner at Fort Delaware

Chalk Level, Va.
Oct. 24th, 1864

Mrs. Rawlings:

Your letter of the 4th inst has been received and contents noticed with care and interest. You seem much distressed about your son Capt. Benjamin Rawlings, of which I am very sorry to hear. I cannot offer you much consolation, for I, too, know a prisoner's life is a hard one. I think Capt. Rawlings is doing as well as most prisoners. He was out of money and tobacco and I believe was needy for clothing. I don't think he has ever received any money from home. I believe he has gotten only two or three letters from home since he has been captured. He has received some supplies from friends in Baltimore, Md., but I do not depend on that, for an order had been issued before I left which prohibited us from receiving anything except by flag of truce.

Our treatment at Ft. Delaware was very rough. We had two meals a day which amounted to less than nine ounces of bread and 5 ounces of meat with little soup for the meal called dinner, which came at 2 o'clock. We had plank floors to rest upon at night with about two blankets to one man. Our water was from Brandywine Creek and occasionally very salty from water backing up from the bay. The officers were in a separate pen from the privates and no communication was allowed by the Yankee authorities, but occasionally we could hear from one another by throwing over a note tied to a rock. This was kept up for some time before the Yankees found it out but they never did suppress it after finding us out.

I wish I could tell you more of our prison life, but I have tried to forget Fort Delaware and everything connected with the name and place. I hope you will excuse my unplain writing, as my hand has been broken and I can scarcely hold a pen. Do not be uneasy about your son. He will get on as well an any prisoner. All you have to do is send him money, tobacco, and clothing by flag of truce, and I think he will be as comfortable as you could expect. Should you want to know any more than is included in this note, address me at Chalk Level, Va., and I will answer with pleasure.

Yours respectfully,
Lieut. P. L. W. Thornton
Chalk Level, Pittsylvania Co., Va.

P.S. Please excuse this paper. It is all that I have. I will write to you again in a few days.

Respectfully,
P. L. W. Thornton

CHAPTER XVI

We Stood Fast to End at Five Forks

There was snow on the ground when I returned to the Petersburg trenches in December to resume command of my company. I found quite a few gaps of those who had fallen during the campaign of 1864. There was nightly skirmishing and picket firing, and we were daily under Butler's big guns. This was the part of the line near the Howlett House.[1] Around the first of February, we were ordered north of the James near Fort Harrison. We camped there near Butler and his colored troops. We remained here until about the first of April, when we were ordered across the river to Petersburg and placed on the right of the line near Hatcher's Run, where Sheridan was extending his lines, flanking Lee's right. From there, we went to the extreme right of the line, striking Sheridan near Dinwiddie Court House, where Sheridan attacked. We lost several in our company killed or wounded. We took up a position the next day at Five Forks, where after repulsing several attacks of Sheridan's cavalry, Warren broke through and rolled up our line on the left. I lost my sword at Five Forks.[2] The next day, in protecting the wagons, we fought the Battle of Sayler's Creek, where we left the field in disorder, losing many men captured.[3] We crossed the bridge over the Appomattox and continued the retreat. I slept while I walked over this railroad bridge.

We were without rations the night before the surrender, so some of the boys killed a hog and cooked it. Having no salt, we were obliged to eat it without salt. That night and the next morning were filled with rumors of the surrender of the Army of Northern Virginia. The artillery was being packed, and the infantry was stacking arms. General Lee in his new uniform was riding across the fields in front, and the whole army was in distress and mortification as the truth was forced upon us that the Army of Northern Virginia was to be surrendered.[4] With recent memories of Yankee prisons, I and one of my men from Kentucky who knew the country concluded to escape through the lines and join General Johnston. The man, originally from Spotsylvania, was named

Buchanan. So, leaving my company in the command of Lt. John Rawlings to surrender on the field, I left with Buchanan to get through the lines, crossing the north side of the James with the intention of going through the mountains to Johnston.[5] After crossing the river, I found that Buchanan did not know the route at all so was forced to go home, which I reached about the third day. My family had refugeed in Hadensville in Goochland County. When I got to the house where my family was staying, I was disheveled, unshaven and glassy-eyed with fatigue and fever. My own little brother, James, did not recognize me and hid in fear behind my mother's skirts.

In conclusion, I wish to bear testimony to Grant's generosity and magnanimous terms to Lee and his Army of Northern Virginia and the way in which he sustained those terms in spite of Yankee renegades in Congress.

CHAPTER XVII

After the War

Excerpts from a Letter Written by Hannah Garlick Rawlings [Sister of John Rawlings] **to Her Sister Clarissa**, Who Spent the Civil War Years With Friends in Pennsylvania

Piedmont, Orange County, Virginia
August 9, 1865

Dear Sister,

You will probably not understand why it is that I am so much in need of clothing -- I will explain. Of course, you know that ever since the commencement of the war, there has been a strict blockade of all our ports. As a consequence, merchandise of every description has been scarce and high. Most of the Virginia ladies, in imitation of our grandmothers during the Revolution, arrayed themselves in homespun. Those who did not find it convenient to follow this fashion -- myself among the number -- imitated the "gude dame" in the "Cotters' Saturday Night," and with the aid of much ingenuity and sundry turnings upside down and inside out, managed to "gae auld claes look amaist as weel's the new." In fact, there was never a time-serving politician who underwent as many metamorphoses as a garment in the hands of a Southern girl during the years 1863 and '4. We had come to regard a patch or a neatly darned rent rather as a badge of distinction than a reproach. It was "a la Confederate" and therefore as it should be. We would not think of spending money upon dress when our soldiers were naked and hungry in the field. I have not purchased anything scarcely for a period of four years and now am in need of *everything*, both underclothing and dresses. I have here in my desk a bundle of "waste paper," a specimen of which I send to you, in the *shape of a $100 bill*. Keep it as a *memento of the Confederacy*. By the way, some of our friends speak of *papering their walls with it*.

You ask me if Mr. Boggs [brother-in-law of Hannah and Clarissa] is among the fortunate few. You shall judge. A year ago he was visited by Sheridan's raiders, who took from him all his horses and mules, his corn, wheat, oats, flour and bacon, leaving his family, consisting of upwards of a hundred persons (white and black) without a morsel to eat. Provisions were then very scarce, but he did manage to get bread and upon that, with milk and vegetables, they subsisted the balance of the year. Whenever any meat could be obtained, it was given to the servants and the white family did without. Since the surrender of our army he has lost a good deal of money and about a hundred Negroes. The last however, I do not look upon as any great misfortune. He has nothing now but his land, a portion of which he will probably be obliged to sell.

When I look back upon the events of the last five months, I sometimes feel as if it could not be reality, and that I have been the victim of some hideous nightmare. From the beginning of Spring, one "unmerciful disaster" after another came upon us till all culminated in the dreadful catastrophe of the 9th of April -- the surrender of Lee's noble army -- that army which had contested the invader almost every foot of ground in our dear old State, and been victorious on a hundred battlefields. Could you have seen some of our soldiers as I saw them after the surrender, it would have wrung your very soul. They seemed almost heartbroken. These who had marched without faltering up to the cannon's mouth and faced death in its most horrid forms, were completely unmanned. I felt as if I could lay my head in the dust and die! For three days after we learned the fate of our devoted army, I don't think there were a dozen words spoken in our house.

The feeling here against the North is intense, tho' smothered. It will never pass away. Mothers will teach their children to abhor the slayers of their fathers and brothers; they will teach it to them from earliest infancy. Had I sons, this is the religion that I would inculcate from the time they could lisp: "Fear God, love the South, and *live to avenge her!*" This is short and easily remembered.

Lillie and Colonel Johnson (only think of Valentine with three stars on his collar) will probably spend the balance of the summer here. Lillie has returned to the Old Dominion with the firm conviction that "there's no place like home." She does not like the far South half so well, though the gay capitol of Florida is a pleasant place enough.

Believe me to be always your most affectionate sister H. G. R.[1]

From the Rawlings Family Genealogy Records

[Ben Rawlings] went West in October, 1866. Crossed the plains with freight wagons from Kansas City to California by way of Arizona. Corralled by Apache Indians for a day and night in Arizona. Lived a year in California. Then went to Nevada and lived 5 years. Mined at White Pine a year and Eureka four years. Returned to Va. in 1874. Was a railroad conductor for two years. (This was on the Norfolk and Western in the Shenandoah Valley, and it was while there that he met my grandmother, the daughter of James E. A. Gibbs, a well-to-do sewing machine inventor, and it was her father who gave them their own farm as a wedding gift. Florence S. Durrance) He then settled on a farm at Raphine, Virginia, in Rockbridge County. He was a deacon in Mt. Carmel Presbyterian Church for 18 years and died of a heart attack in his pew in the church on October 18, 1908.

Letter from Ben Rawlings to Florence Gibbs, 1875

Section 15 C.S. Railway
Oct. 1st, 75

My darling,

Your sweet letters dated respectfully the 9th and 24th came safely to hand. I am gratified to know that you are *assured* of an escort to the springs, knowing the loneliness you would undoubtedly feel in traveling so far alone. I was in Knoxville on the 16th inst. and had my photo taken to send as you suggested. Leaving instructions with the artist to forward them to me at Wartburg when completed. They have not come yet, & my delay in answering your letter was owing to this fact, as I wished to send you my picture. By the same mail & bearing the same date as yours of the 9th inst. I received a kind and friendly letter from your father. In which he gave his unqualified approval to our engagement. I answered it at once, addressing him at Providence.

You must send me your picture, sweetheart mine, before you leave on your trip. I want to see how you are looking now. I have two pictures of you now, one in my trunk, the other in

100

my *heart*. The former I might lose. The latter I *cannot*. Except with my life. It is engraven *too deep*.

Darling, I have not the time this morning to write you a longer letter. Although I have much to say to you. Be sure & write me before you leave home and directly you arrive at the Springs. Your dear letters are my only sunshine. It seems so long to look forward to before I may be able to see your sweet face again. I dreamed of you last night. Dreamed of traveling with sister and you on a long journey & a large crowd and in the confusion of changing from steamboats to stage coaches I lost you. Leaving my sister in a safe place, I ran to find you, and after a long and weary search midst the crowd, who seemed to gaze on me as if I were an escaped lunatic -- I found you in a deserted and broken down *stage coach, waiting for me,* so quietly and patiently that I could not resist the temptation of taking a sweet kiss. Before we could explain I awoke. Leaving me at a loss to conjecture our destination. Good Bye, sweetheart, Good Bye. May angels guard you from all evil and unhappiness is the prayer of

Your devoted lover,
B. C. Rawlings

From the Rawlings Family Scrapbooks

By Rev. A. H. Hamilton, at Raphine, the residence of the bride's father, on the morning of the 10th May [1876] Capt. B. C. RAWLINGS, of Spotsylvania County, Va., and Miss FLORENCE V. GIBBS, daughter of James E. A. Gibbs, of Rockbridge County.

From the Richmond *Dispatch*
May, 1891

Who Was the Youngest That Actually Served?

An Ex-Congressman's Career

Burkeville, Va., May 21, 1891

*To the Editor of the **Dispatch**:*

Please state that my father, ex-Congressman William E. Gaines, served in the Confederate army four years and seventeen days actively and continuously before he attained his twenty-first birthday. He was born August 30, 1844; enlisted April 16, 1861, and surrendered with Johnston May, 1865.

Battles fought: First Manassas, Yorktown, Williamsburg, Seven Pines, Gaines's Mill, Frazer's Farm, Second Manassas, Sharpsburg, Fredericksburg, Cold Harbor, Gettysburg, Kingston, Fort Fisher, and Bentonville.

I claim the marbles on all-the-war, all-around, youngest soldier.

Truly and respectfully, W. E. Gaines, Jr.

The First Virginia Volunteer

To the Editor of the Dispatch:

Mr. W. E. Gaines, Jr., will have to "pass over the marbles" to Captain B. C. Rawlings of Raphine, Va., as the youngest all-the-war soldier. Captain Rawlings was born January 9, 1845, and was reared in Spotsylvania County, Va. He left home December 24, 1860, for Charleston, South Carolina, and enlisted the first week in January, 1861, in the First Regiment, South Carolina Volunteers, Colonel Maxcy Gregg commanding (who was afterwards General Gregg and who was killed at Fredericksburg in 1862) Company A, Captain D. B. Miller commanding. The regiment was then guarding Sullivan's Island. He was on Morris Island during the bombardment of Fort Sumter, and saw the fire from the signal gun and the white flag raised at Sumter. He came to Richmond with his regiment the last of April, 1861, and was transferred at his own request to Company D, Thirtieth Virginia Regiment to serve his native state according to a promise made him by Colonel Gregg when he enlisted that he should be transferred as soon as Virginia had need of troops. Colonel Gregg, in his discharge, recommended him for a commissioned officer. He was appointed orderly sergeant immediately and elected first lieutenant at the reorganization of the army in 1862. He was lieutenant commanding his company at Malvern Hill, Harper's Ferry, Sharpsburg, and Fredericksburg, when he was only seventeen and a half years old, and was promoted to the captaincy on the field at the siege of Suffolk in April, 1863. He was captured November 27, 1863, and starved at Point Lookout and Fort Delaware eleven months, was exchanged and joined his company in the trenches around Petersburg, where he remained until General Lee's retreat to Appomattox. He participated in the battles of Dinwiddie Court House, Five Forks, and Sayler's Creek and surrendered with General Lee the day he was twenty years and three months old, having served his country four years and three months, or from the occupation of Fort Sumter to the surrender at Appomattox.

I also claim for Captain Rawlings that he was the first Virginia volunteer for the defense of the Confederacy. Let us hear from the others. I would like very much to have the latter claim settled definitely.

Virginia

From M. S. Funkhouser to Ben Rawlings

B. C. Rawlings, Esq., Raphine, Va.

Dear Sir:

Will you kindly tell me your age and the circumstances and facts connected with your enlistment in the Confederate service.

I write this at the instance of R. B. Murphy, who has a medal from Congress for being the youngest enlisted boy in the Federal army.

Mr. Murphy desires to exchange photographs with the youngest Confederate soldier, who served three years or more.

Truly, M. P. Funkhouser

Benjamin Cason Rawlings

Photograph courtesy of John Brake.

From the Fredericksburg *Free Lance*
August 30, 1892

Captain Ben Rawlings

We had a pleasant visit from Capt. Benjamin Rawlings, a former citizen of this county, who, since the war,has resided in the beautiful Valley of Virginia, and is now a prosperous citizen of the county of Rockbridge. Capt. Rawlings is a brother of our esteemed fellow citizen, James E. Rawlings, and is a genial Virginia gentleman. Capt. Ben, as he was familiarly called, was the youngest captain in the 30th Virginia Regiment, and at the early age of eighteen years commanded Company D of that regiment. At the outbreak of the war, Captain Rawlings, then a stripling of sixteen years, impatient at Virginia's delay, went to South Carolina and enlisted in the 1st South Carolina Infantry under Colonel (afterwards General) Maxcy Gregg and came to Virginia with that regiment. Upon the arrival of his regiment in Virginia he was transferred to the 30th Virginia Regiment Infantry, then being formed at this place and was made 1st Sergeant of company D, and the history of that company and regiment is Ben Rawlings' war record. There was no more gallant soldier in the regiment, and no one possessed, in a higher degree, the confidence of officers and men than did the gallant young captain.

He is kindly and affectionately remembered by his old comrades, who scarcely recognize in the stalwart form he now has the *la petite* captain of thirty years ago.

106

Excerpts from an Article in the Fredericksburg *Free Lance*
September 16, 1892

Thirty Years Ago

The 30th Virginia Regiment at the Battle of Sharpsburg

Tomorrow, September 17, is the thirtieth anniversary of the battle of Sharpsburg, or Antietam, as the Federals designate it. In this battle the Thirtieth Virginia Regiment, composed of three companies from this city, four from Caroline, one from Spotsylvania, one from Stafford, and one from King George, received its first baptismal of fire and was nearly annihilated. The regiment went into the fight 295 strong, and the killed and wounded numbered two-thirds of those engaged -- 57 being killed, and 148 wounded. The flag of the regiment had fifteen balls shot through it, and one corner shot off. The flag was carried from the field by Lieut. R. T. Knox, and is now in possession of Maury Camp.

As a matter of interest, we publish a list of the killed and wounded, which we copy from the *Virginia Herald* of September 26 [1862], which has been in the possession of Mrs. Kauffman Hirsh for thirty years.

Company D -- Wounded: Lieut. Rawlings, slightly; John Willoughby, slightly in arm, Sergeant Gordon. [Ben Rawlings notes under this article in one of the family scrapbooks that the list of killed and wounded for Company D is incomplete.]

The members of the regiment lost all their clothing, blankets, camp equipage, etc. The Third Arkansas Regiment, which was in the same brigade with the 30th, also suffered severely, and wearing apparel and bed clothing were contributed by our citizens after the battle and sent to the two regiments.

From a Rockbridge County Newspaper, 1894

An "April Fool" at Raphine

(Correspondence of the County News)

April 3, 1894 -- There was quite an exciting and also amusing scene, to those who were in the secret, at the residence of Captain Ben Rawlings last night. The captain stated in the presence of his family early in the evening that he had received a telegram announcing the fact that burglars had been operating around Greenville, and from the information obtained, they might be expected in this section pretty soon, perhaps that night, and that they would make a raid on him. Sure enough, about 10 o'clock, a noise was heard about the corn-crib. The captain called to his son Emery, a youth of about sixteen, to get his gun and to Charlie Chittum, a young man living with him, to get a sabre in the room, which they did, and forth they sallied, determined to give the bur-ga-lers a warm reception. On reaching the yard two objects were discerned in front of the crib whilst a noise as if some one was endeavoring to break in was kept up. The captain told Emery to let them have it, which he proceeded forthwith to do. On firing his guns down went one of the figures, and immediately groans were heard as if someone in mortal agony. Captain told Emery to take the sabre and go and dispatch him. Emery said, Oh! no, I can't go there. He then told Chittum to go and spear them. Forward with a bound Charlie went and reaching the standing bur-ga-ler, he gave him two thrusts and down he went. But the moaning continued and sounded as though it was in the rear of the crib. Around the crib went the boys determined to make finis of the whole set. But not being able to find anyone they returned to view those already hors du combat. On examination as to their identity, they were found to be dummies. The captain very complacently remarked, "Well, Charles you promised me last year that I should never make an April fool of you again." One incident connected with the affair yesterday (Monday): Mrs. R. was having some mending done, and she thought of a pair of pants of the captain's which with a little repair, would serve him a good summer but she could not find them anywhere. This morning they are not worth repairing so true was Emery's aim.

From the Fredericksburg *Star*
August, 1897

A Distinguished Confederate Among Us

Capt. Benjamin C. Rawlings, of Rockbridge County, is the guest of his brother, Mr. James R. Rawlings. Captain Rawlings commanded Company D, Thirtieth Virginia Regiment, C.S.A., during the war. The local name of this company was the "Mt. Pleasant Riflemen," and was recruited mostly from Spotsylvania County. Captain Rawlings enjoys the further distinction of being the first man to volunteer from his native State in behalf of the Confederate cause: He left Virginia before she seceded, and, making his way to South Carolina, enlisted for the war. Capt. Rawlings comes to our section periodically to visit his relatives and shake hands with those who shared the hardships and privations of the four years of the war.

Captain Benjamin C. Rawlings

The congregation of Mt. Carmel Church, Augusta County, Va., was greatly shocked and distressed just at the beginning of services Sunday morning, the 18th of October [1908], by the sudden death in his pew of Captain Benjamin C. Rawlings.

He was born the 9th of January, 1845, and was reared in Spotsylvania County, Va. He came to Rockbridge county as a contractor on the Valley Railroad about the year 1872. In May, 1876, he married Miss Florence V. Gibbs, the eldest daughter of the late James E. A. Gibbs, of Raphine, Va., and became a citizen of that community.

Capt. Rawlings was distinguished as a Confederate soldier in more ways than one. Not willing to wait until there was a call for troops in Virginia, without his father's knowledge, he left home December 24, 1860, for Charleston, S.C., and there enlisted the first week in January, 1861, in the First Regiment of South Carolina Volunteers, Colonel (afterwards General) Maxcy Gregg commanding. From Morris Island he saw the flash of the signal gun for opening the fire upon Ft. Sumter, and saw the white flag go up when that famous fort surrendered.

When his regiment came to Richmond in April, 1861, he was transferred, at his own request,

110

to Company D, Thirtieth Virginia Infantry, to serve his native state. He rapidly rose from one rank to another until, at the age of seventeen and one-half years he was lieutenant commanding his company; and when but little over eighteen, was promoted to the captaincy, on the field, at the siege of Suffolk, for gallant conduct.

After a period of eleven months in prison, he joined his company again in the trenches around Petersburg, the last terrible winter of the war, and was with General Lee in the retreat to Appomattox and at the surrender the 9th of April, 1865, the day he was twenty years and three months old. He was the first Virginian to volunteer in the service of the Southern Confederacy.

As a citizen, he took a deep interest in all matters affecting the welfare of the county, the State and the nation. He was a genial, high-toned gentleman, and was highly esteemed in the community where he lived for thirty-two years.

He joined the Baptist Church, the church of his ancestors, in his early life, but became a member of Mt. Carmel Presbyterian Church soon after settling at Raphine, and was elected deacon in 1890.

As a Christian; he was consistent; as a member and officer of the church, he was faithful. He was a strong friend and supporter of his pastor. He was a visitor of the sick, a helper of the poor, a personal worker among the unconverted, a strong advocate of world-wide evangelism -- an *all-round good man.*

Brave Soldier Heart! Thy work is done,
Thy glorious crown is this:
Thy master calls thee home to realms
of everlasting bliss.

Brave Soldier Heart! The fight is o'er,
Life's din and noise of strife
Are all forgot, since thou art come
To everlasting life!

Inscription on Ben Rawlings' Tombstone,
Mt. Carmel Presbyterian Church,
Augusta County, Virginia

Benjamin C. Rawlings

Captain of

Co. D, 30th Va. Inf.

Corse's Brigade

Pickett's Div.

Longstreet's Corps

Born Jan. 9, 1845

Died Oct. 18, 1908

EXPLANATORY NOTES

Chapter 1:

1. The South Carolina ordinance of secession was signed on Dec. 20, 1860. This news spread quickly by telegraph and was printed in the Fredericksburg *News* on December 22.

On December 26, U.S. General Robert Anderson moved his troops from Sullivan's Island, a small peninsula vulnerable to land attack, to Fort Sumter. Secessionists were outraged; they believed this action to be a violation of President James Buchanan's guarantees of no changes in the status of the federal garrison at Charleston.

2. Weldon, North Carolina, was an important railroad junction. Goldsboro is approximately eighty miles south of Weldon in the coastal plain area of North Carolina.

3. The *Star of the West*, a merchant steamer loaded with additional men and ammunition for Fort Sumter, was fired on by the South Carolina troops on January 9, 1861, Ben Rawlings' sixteenth birthday.

4. "Broken down" means exhausted. "Run his face" is a variation of "to run one's board," which means to leave without paying for board.

5. The lack of hospitality which Rawlings encountered is similar to difficulties described by Frederick Law Olmstead in *The Cotton Kingdom*. In 1860, this rural, isolated part of North Carolina had no plank roads or towns of any size on this route along the railroad tracks to Wilmington.

6. In the *Oxford Dictionary*, one meaning of "cobbler" is "a clumsy workman, a mere botcher." A "cobble text" is a "preacher who deals clumsily and unskillfully with a text."

7. John Preston, a Virginian educated at the University of Virginia and Harvard, had made a fortune from his Louisiana sugar plantation. An ardent secessionist and skilled orator, he was married to the sister of Wade Hampton, a wealthy South Carolinian who later headed Hampton's Legion of cavalry in the Army of Northern Virginia. At the beginning of the Civil War, Preston was on the staff of P. G. T. Beauregard and later headed the Bureau of Conscription. Preston and his family figure prominently in Mary Boykin Chesnut's *A Diary from Dixie*.

8. Edmund Ruffin, an extreme secessionist, was a Virginia agricultural reformer who had long advocated independence for the South. He attended the secession conventions in South Carolina, Florida, and North Carolina in an effort to persuade those states to leave the union. Most likely, Rawlings was introduced to Ruffin by John Preston, who knew Ruffin well.

Chapter II:

1. Maxcy Gregg, of Columbia, South Carolina, a lawyer and scholar of considerable reputation, had been appointed colonel of the South Carolina Volunteers, an infantry regiment authorized by the South Carolina secession convention to serve the state for six months. Gregg had been a major in the Mexican War, but his main interest in the ante-bellum years was political. As the consummate fire-eating Southern politician, Gregg's opinions were extreme even in South Carolina; he advocated unilateral secession by South Carolina and the reopening of the African slave trade as early as 1852. Thus, South Carolina's secession was a goal toward which Gregg had worked for nearly a decade.

2. Company A, the Richland Rifles, was from Columbia, which is in Richland County, S.C.

3. Sullivan's Island and Morris Island were the two land areas nearest Fort Sumter, which was surrounded by water in Charleston Harbor. Cummings Point, the spit of land at the tip of Morris Island, was only 1,250 yards from Fort Sumter. The artillery

batteries on Cummings Point were the most important military installations on Morris Island; the infantry was present in case Union gunboats landed men on the island in an effort to take the batteries from the rear. During the months before the Fort Sumter bombardment, additional batteries were built so that the South Carolinians could fire at Fort Sumter's poorly-fortified rear. The fort's designers had not expected the fort to be attacked from the land side.

4. According to the Charleston *Daily Courier* of January 4, 1861, the lieutenants of the Darlington Guards were D. G. McIntosh, T. A. Sanders, J. W. Norwood, and J. E. Nettles.

5. F.F.V. is an abbreviation for "First Families of Virginia." A member or descendant of one of the first families to settle in Virginia is called an F.F.V., sometimes in admiration, sometimes in derision.

6. Rawlings' avowal not to "show the white feather" refers to the white feathers in a game bird's tail, visible when the bird is fleeing its enemy. Rawlings was determined never to have his courage and honor questioned, even though he might be killed.

7. Lincoln's inauguration and his decision to reinforce the Fort Sumter garrison brought to a head the smoldering crisis. On April 7, all food supplies from Charleston to Fort Sumter were ordered cut off; the last battery of the island defenses had been completed a few days earlier. The Morris Island troops were ready for a fight.

8. Rawlings discredits the tradition that Edmund Ruffin fired the first shot at Fort Sumter. Ruffin, sixty-seven years old in 1861, had been named an honorary member of the Palmetto Guards, the unit which manned the Cummings Point batteries. Ruffin was asked by members of that unit to fire the first shot from the Cummings Point batteries. In his diary, Ruffin stated that he fired his gun after a signal gun was fired from Fort Johnson on James Island. Civil War historian Bruce Catton states in *The Coming Fury* that the gun fired after the James Island signal gun

could have been from Fort Moultrie, James Island, or Cummings's Point. A controversy has long surrounded the firing of the first shot at Fort Sumter. See Martin Abbott, "The First Shot at Fort Sumter," *Civil War History*, III, (March, 1957), 41-45.

9. In his diary, Edmund Ruffin did not mention falling in the sand and heading for a "healthier climate." He said that during the bombardment, his duty was to look over the parapet of the Cummings Point battery to determine the direction and accuracy of the battery's firing and to warn of balls coming toward the battery from the Fort Sumter guns. Perhaps Ben Rawlings was one of the "others of unemployed soldiers (for the time) who afterwards stood with me to indulge their curiosity, which caused Col. De Saussure, about 1 o'clock, to order all of us down, lest we should attract the notice and fire of Major Anderson." See Ruffin, "The First Shot at Fort Sumter," 81.

10. Louis T. Wigfall, a former United States senator from Texas, was a native of South Carolina. An early, ardent secessionist, he was in no way authorized to arrange the surrender of Fort Sumter. He did so on his own and thereby caused Major Anderson and authorized Confederate representatives great embarrassment. Wigfall and his wife are often mentioned in *A Diary from Dixie*.

11. R. H. Rawlings' letter of April 3, 1861, to his brother James Boswell Rawlings in Virginia reflects the contrast in sentiment between the Gulf cotton states and four states where union sentiment was still strong -- Virginia, North Carolina, Tennessee, and Arkansas. In February, 1861, Georgia, Alabama, Florida, Mississippi, Louisiana, and Texas had joined with South Carolina to form the Confederate States of America. The Confederate capitol was at that time Montgomery, Alabama, which explains why R. H. Rawlings offered to use his influence in Montgomery to obtain a promotion for Ben Rawlings.

12. Many citizens of the new Confederacy were just as naively optimistic as was R. H. Rawlings. They expected to be

allowed to form their own country without fighting a war. Cotton was booming, and they saw nothing but prosperity ahead.

13. "Zach" was Zachary Herndon Rawlings, Ben's older brother, who married Betty Baker Rowe in December, 1960. Nannie (Nancy) and Lucy were Ben's sisters, Ben also had a younger brother, James.

Chapter III:

1. The violence of Fort Sumter brought about the result desired by the Confederacy: Virginia passed a secession ordinance on April 17, and the other upper South states followed.

2. The realities of war and human nature again were impressed upon the artless Ben Rawlings. His naiveté and Virginia hubris were such that he was amazed when his fellow soldiers were not full of enthusiasm "to go to the succor of Old Virginia." The South Carolinians had volunteered for six months solely for the defense of their state; they were not obligated to leave South Carolina. In their reluctance to do so, they were like many other Southerners whose first loyalty was to their state rather than to the nation as a whole, be it the United States or the Confederacy.

3. Alexander Cheves Haskell, assistant adjutant on Maxcy Gregg's staff, wrote that the South Carolina soldiers felt a special pride, since they had already proven their mettle under fire; as the seasoned "Morris Island" troops, they thought it important to exercise a steadying influence on the raw recruits they would find in Virginia. Alex Haskell is another South Carolinian often mentioned in *A Diary from Dixie*.

4. Uncle Herndon Frazier was a Baptist minister and husband of Ben Rawlings' Aunt Martha. They lived in Orange County, Virginia. Ben's home, "Green Hill," was in western Spotsylvania County, not far from Parker's Store on the Orange Plank Road.

5. Captain Valentine Johnson's family lived at "Forest Hill," a few miles south of Ben Rawlings' home. Johnson refused to be a candidate for election as captain of Company D in 1862. He then became superintendent of the Florida Military Academy in Tallahassee, a position which he held until the end of the war.

6. Since Ben Rawlings' family had lived in Spotsylvania County since the early 1700's, it was fitting that he join the Mount Pleasant Rifles, which became Company D of the Thirtieth Virginia Infantry Regiment. A small company recruited almost entirely from the county, its roots were deeper than those of the other Spotsylvania companies, which drew primarily from the town of Fredericksburg. Because the history of the Mount Pleasant Rifles could be traced back to Revolutionary days, Company D represented the indigenous Spotsylvania County unit.

Chapter IV:

1. Northern Virginia, bounded by the navigable waters of the Potomac and Rappahannock Rivers, was vulnerable to naval attack. The Potomac estuaries of Occoquan Creek, Potomac Creek, and Aquia Creek had to be protected by shore batteries and supporting ground troops.

2. French leave means leaving without permission.

3. The old Tump Fishery was a large commercial fishing establishment which had burned in 1848.

4. The artillery exchange which occurred while Rawlings and his friends were fishing took place on May 31, 1861. The *Thomas Freeborn*, a Union side-wheeled steamer, fired fourteen shells at the Aquia Creek Railroad battery. The shells were too light to damage the battery, which replied with twelve shells.

5. On June 1, the *Freeborn* and the *Pawnee* shelled the Confederate batteries and the woods in the rear. The bombardment lasted five hours with little damage on either side.

6. The presence of the Thirtieth Virginia at Marlboro Point protected Potomac Creek and placed more troops near Mathias Point, where the Confederates expected an attack. On June 25, the Federals landed at Mathias Point and tried to erect a battery. Company H of the Thirtieth, already at Mathias Point, drove off the Federals before the rest of the regiment arrived. The captain of the *Freeborn* was killed.

7. Civil War soldiers suffered greatly from contagious diseases, especially the rural Southern troops who had acquired less immunity than soldiers from urban areas.

8. The Thirtieth Virginia marched to Manassas along with the 6,000 other troops under the command of Brigadier General Theophilus H. Holmes. The men of the regiment experienced virtually no fighting. In the morning, their part of the line was not engaged; in the afternoon, they were ordered to reinforce the left, but the Federals had begun to retreat before they arrived on the scene.

Chapter V:

1. During the winter of 1862, General Holmes, a North Carolinian, divided his troops into brigades; the Thirtieth Virginia became part of the Second Brigade of General John G. Walker, a former captain in the United States army whom Joseph E. Johnston called "a very competent officer." Also in the Second Brigade were three North Carolina regiments, the Third Arkansas, Cooke's Battery, and Walker's Battery. It could not have pleased the Thirtieth Virginia to be in a brigade with no other Virginia infantry.

2. "Found your mule" is a variation of the Civil War nonsense term, "Here's your mule."

3. Sally and Mary Partington were two of the best-known actresses in the Confederate theater. Both were accomplished dancers, and Sally was praised as a comedienne. "Maryland, My

Maryland," was one of many songs written for theaters in the South. The words exhort Maryland, a border state with many Southern sympathizers, to become part of the Confederacy.

Chapter VI:

1. An intense re-enlistment campaign was conducted in all of the Southern armies. In December, 1861, the Confederate Congress passed the Furlough and Bounty Act, which provided a bounty of $50 and a sixty day furlough for enlisted men and noncommissioned officers. The soldiers had to agree to serve for the duration of the war or a maximum of three years. Even though the soldiers could change companies, arm of service, and elect new officers, less than half agreed to re-enlist. In April, 1862, the conscription act became law, and many men then enlisted or volunteered rather than become known as a conscript. Ben Rawlings is listed on the Bounty Pay and Receipt roll of February 8.

2. Military events soon brought the Thirtieth Virginia back to the Old Dominion. Union General George B. McClellan began his Peninsula Campaign on April 4. By the end of May, he had inched his way from Yorktown to within five miles of Richmond. Brigadier General Irvin McDowell had another Union army north of Fredericksburg. More and more regiments were taken from North Carolina to meet the double threat in Virginia, although General Holmes complained on April 27 that he would be left "with but two brigades (Walker's and Branch's) that can be at all relied on if Burnside advances." The Thirtieth Virginia, as part of Walker's Brigade, was thus one of the last units to be transferred to Virginia.

3. The Thirtieth Virginia left Goldsboro by train around noon and reached Petersburg at daybreak on Wednesday, May 28, after a safe but disagreeable ride on old, leaky freight cars. The men were "well-soaked."

4. The regimental roster lists three privates named Brumley in the Thirtieth Virginia, but Rawlings' reference to Brumley's extreme youth makes it likely the R. B. Brumley is the

picket described. There were also three men named Harris: George F., John A., and Thomas A.

5. The *Oxford Dictionary* defines "Egyptian Darkness" as "intense darkness," a Biblical reference to the plague of darkness described in Exodus 10:22.

6. This excerpt from the Lizzie Maxwell Alsop Journal is used by permission of the Virginia Historical Society.

Chapter VII:

1. General Johnston planned to attack the part of McClellan's army that was north of the Chickahominy River before McClellan and McDowell could join forces. The need for additional men compelled the Confederates to strip the vital James River defenses of troops, including the Thirtieth Virginia. General Walker's men were in Richmond by early morning on June 1. Johnston was wounded at Seven Pines, and Robert E. Lee assumed command of the Confederate forces.

2. On June 25, the Seven Days battles began as Lee sought to destroy McClellan before he could reach his new base on the James River. The next day, Walker's Brigade again was ordered north of the James. The battle at Gaines Mill took place June 27.

3. Late in the afternoon of June 30, an officer of engineers informed General Holmes that the Federals were retreating over Malvern Hill and recommended that Holmes place his artillery so as to dispute the enemy's retreat. Holmes then sent six rifled guns supported by the Thirtieth Virginia "to the point indicated, some two miles down the river road," an advanced position isolated from other Confederate troops. General Lee himself rode to Holmes' command and learned that the guns and one regiment had been sent forward. Lee ordered Holmes to bring the rest of his division to support the batteries and to open fire on the Federals on Malvern Hill.

4. Unfortunately for the Confederates, the Federals were not retreating over Malvern Hill but by midafternoon were well established there. By the time the Confederates reached their position, the Federals had thirty-six guns, some of them long-range, and several siege guns on Malvern Hill. In addition, gunboats on the James opened fire with shells known as "lamp-posts" because of their size and appearance. These "roaring, howling, gunboat shells...had a wonderful effect upon the nervous system."

5. The intense artillery fire described by Rawlings took place on Monday, June 30, at the battle of Malvern Cliff or Turkey Bridge. Major infantry fighting also took place that day in an engagement known as Frayser's Farm or White Oak Swamp.

6. July 1, the day after the Thirtieth Virginia was under the fierce artillery fire, desperate fighting took place at Malvern Hill. Casualties were heavy on both sides. This battle ended the Peninsula Campaign; Lee had kept McClellan out of Richmond, but the Federal army was intact and had reached the new base on the James.

Chapter VIII:

1. Ben Rawlings and his regiment spent the next several weeks in relative inactivity south of the James. Jackson went to northern Virginia to oppose General John Pope, who had replaced McDowell. Pope remarked that he had come from the army in the west, where his headquarters had been in the saddle. Abraham Lincoln said that Pope had his headquarters where his hindquarters ought to be.

2. The Thirtieth Virginia was still part of Walker's Division of the Dept. of North Carolina, now under the command of D. H. Hill. On August 20, these forces were ordered to northern Virginia to join Jackson and Lee. McClellan had moved his army from the Peninsula to Aquia Creek and Alexandria.

3. The Battle of Cedar Mountain took place August 9. On August 29 and 30, Lee and Jackson defeated Pope at Second Manassas, thereby relieving Richmond. Lee was on the offensive.

4. The Thirtieth Virginia marched to Richmond and took the train north as far as Rapidan Station, where "the burned bridge at that point put an end to the effortless marching on wheels." The men left the Rapidan on September 1 and reached Leesburg September 6. The band played "Maryland, My Maryland" as the regiment crossed the Potomac.

5. The Federal garrison in Harper's Ferry was a threat to Lee's offensive plans. On September 10, Walker's Division was sent to Harper's Ferry to cooperate with Jackson and Major General Lafayette McLaws. By September 14, Walker's Division occupied Loudoun Heights; McLaws had seized Maryland Heights; and Jackson's infantry had approached Harper's Ferry from the north, thus surrounding the town.

6. On September 15, a heavy mist obscured Harper's Ferry from the artillery on Loudoun Heights until eight A.M., when the Confederates opened fire. The Union garrison hoisted the white flag around 9:30 A.M.

7. The Federal soldiers were "indignant beyond expression" that they were forced to surrender. They blamed their commander, Miles, for failure to show initiative; they blamed McClellan for not relieving them; they blamed Maj. Gen. William B. Franklin for his slowness in coming to their aid.

8. Other plunderers that day in Harper's Ferry were Ben Rawlings' old friends in the First South Carolina Volunteers, now part of Lieutenant General A. P. Hill's Light Division.

9. Jackson was cheered not only by the Confederates but also by the captured Union soldiers, who "rushed to the road, threw up their hats, cheered, roared, and bellowed, as even Jackson's own troops had scarcely ever done." No doubt they wished for a general as skilled as Jackson.

Chapter IX:

1. On September 13, McClellan had an opportunity to destroy Lee's divided army. The famous copy of Lee's Special Orders No. 191 was found, wrapped around a few cigars, by Union troops. These orders, which pinpointed the location of every Confederate division, prompted McClellan to move somewhat more swiftly than usual but still too slowly to trap Lee and defeat each portion of his army piecemeal. By September 16, Lee was able to assemble most of his army along Antietam Creek near Sharpsburg. A. P. Hill was still in Harper's Ferry.

2. Early on the morning of September 17, Walker's men were on the extreme right of the Confederate line, south of Sharpsburg, in position to cover the ford over Antietam Creek and to support Brigadier General Robert Toombs, whose small force thwarted during the day the many attempts of Major General Ambrose F. Burnside to cross the stone bridge which came to bear his name.

3. Walker's Division hurried from the extreme right to approximately the middle of the battle line. Around 10 A.M. they neared the Dunkard Church on the Hagerstown Pike, close to two pieces of woods known thereafter as the West Woods and the East Woods. Between the woods was the Cornfield, where Jackson's and Hooker's men had fought desperately earlier that morning. The cornfield Ben Rawlings mentions was well to the south of this more famous cornfield. The Battle of Antietam was fought on farm land, and there were numerous cultivated fields of corn and other crops.

4. The Thirtieth Virginia, along with the Forty-eighth and Forty-sixth North Carolina regiments, advanced across the Hagerstown Pike toward a ridge on the Mumma farm. Their line of battle extended from the Dunkard Church south in the direction of the Sunken Road, scene of intense fighting later in the day.

5. The official battle reports claim that the division "advanced in splendid style, firing and cheering as they went." They emerged from the woods, and then the Thirtieth Virginia and the Forty-eighth North Carolina "dashed forward in gallant style" across the open fields until they reached the post and rail fences. There they became bunched up, unable to maneuver, and became perfect targets for the artillery and the Ohio regiments on top of the hill. The men had to retreat in close proximity to the enemy, "the most dangerous course in war." Colonel E. D. Hall of the Forty-sixth North Carolina saw the folly of such an impetuous charge and ordered his regiment to seek protection behind rail breastworks. Hall watched the unfortunate Thirtieth Virginia and Forty-eighth North Carolina in their desperate struggle and thought the troops "behaved as well as any troops could who were in such an exposed and fatal position."

6. Ben Rawlings' criticism that the supports "refused to come up" is somewhat harsh. The responsibility for the disastrous charge lay with the Arkansas colonel, Vannoy H. Manning, who imprudently led the Thirtieth Virginia and the Forty-eighth North Carolina "without any reconnaissance or support on either flank" into withering artillery and infantry fire. Manning's own regiment, the Third Arkansas, had been sent to the part of the line which became known as Bloody Lane.

7. In his official report, General Walker unfairly criticized the Thirtieth Virginia. He ignored the regiment's heavy casualties and said that "owing to some unaccountable misunderstanding of orders" the regiment left the field and "was not again engaged during the day." In later years, however, Walker described the regiment's behavior more favorably when he said that the Virginians were "fearfully cut up" and escaped "annihilation by a timely retreat to the cover of the wood."

Chapter X:

1. Ben Rawlings and his fellow soldiers probably did not realize in the fall of 1862 that the tide of Confederate hope for

125

ultimate victory had crested along Antietam Creek and was receding even as the Army of Northern Virginia lay in camp near Winchester and Culpeper. Shelby Foote stated that at Antietam, the "troops Lee lost were the best he had -- the best he could ever hope to have." Foreign intervention and recognition were no longer realistic possibilities; the army's cool reception in Maryland showed that the border states were unwilling to risk support of the South; most important, the Emancipation Proclamation, issued after Antietam, gave to the North the moral initiative and changed the purpose of the war. Antietam was indeed "a forecast of disaster for the Confederacy."

2. In the fall of 1862, the Thirtieth Virginia became officially part of the Army of Northern Virginia. The regiment was assigned to Corse's Brigade, Pickett's Division, and Longstreet's Corps. The other regiments in the brigade were all from Virginia, a change which pleased the men of the Thirtieth.

3. When Ambrose E. Burnside succeeded McClellan as commander of the Army of the Potomac on November 7, he determined to move directly to Richmond and believed he could cross the Rappahannock at Fredericksburg unopposed if his army moved quickly. Unfortunately for Burnside and his men, by the time his pontoon bridges had arrived and he had at length decided to cross the river, the Confederates were well-entrenched on the high ground around Fredericksburg.

4. The evacuation of Fredericksburg was one of the first and most massive civilian displacements of the war. Some refugees went to the homes of friends and relatives in the county; others camped out in the December weather; several hundred stayed at the Salem Baptist Church, a few miles west of Fredericksburg on the Orange Turnpike. As the December wind rattled the limbs of the leafless trees, the homeless civilians huddled around numerous fires in the churchyard. Ambulances full of wounded soldiers clogged the road. War had come to Spotsylvania County.

5. Pickett's Division was on Telegraph Hill, the center of the Confederate line. This high ground was not attacked by the

Union forces, but the men posted there could see the battle unfolding below them. On December 11, Confederate sharpshooters harassed Union engineers while they tried to place the pontoon bridges across the river. The next day, the Mississippi troops of General William Barksdale, in spite of a heavy Union bombardment of the town, skillfully delayed the advance of the Federals through Fredericksburg. When Burnside was finally ready to advance on December 13, his unfortunate men were slaughtered as they made many courageous but suicidal assaults on the strong Confederate positions. The ill-used Union army withdrew to the north side of the Rappahannock on December 15.

6. Confederate camp humor often focused on anyone, particularly a stranger, who wore something unusual or obviously new.

Chapter XI:

1. Snowball fights were a popular winter sport in the Southern armies. These caricatures of actual battles were conducted according to army rules with such enthusiasm that casualties -- black eyes, bruises, and even broken bones -- sometimes resulted.

Chapter XII:

1. Longstreet, given a semi-independent command in Southeastern Virginia, left Spotsylvania County in February, 1863. The divisions of Pickett and Hood went into camp near Petersburg on the south side of the James. In March, as part of Longstreet's plan to invest Suffolk, the Thirtieth Virginia was sent to Ivor Station on the Norfolk and Petersburg Railroad, two miles from the Blackwater River and approximately twenty-five miles from Suffolk. In April, Longstreet advanced toward Suffolk; the Federal troops fell back to the city's defenses, and the siege began.

127

2. General Joe Hooker, the latest commander of the Army of the Potomac, crossed the Rappahannock on April 28. Lee ordered Longstreet north to unite with the rest of the army, but the Battle of Chancellorsville began May 2, before Pickett and Hood withdrew from Suffolk. The Thirtieth Virginia remained in camp near Richmond until May 15.

Chapter XIII:

1. Lee wanted Corse's Brigade with him during the Gettysburg Campaign, but Jefferson Davis was concerned, perhaps overly so, with protecting the rail communications to Richmond. Only after the Battle of Gettysburg was Corse ordered to rejoin Pickett. The Thirtieth Virginia arrived in Winchester on July 13, where they met the rest of Pickett's Division.

2. The Thirtieth Virginia spent the rest of the summer in camp first near Culpeper and then in Verdiersville, a village in Orange County not far from Ben Rawlings' home. During the fall of 1863, the regiment moved, both by foot and by rail, between Petersburg, Western Virginia, and East Tennessee. Federal forces had occupied Knoxville and threatened to advance into Virginia along the railroad lines. The regiment was in Zollicoffer, Tennessee, by September 16 and remained in that state until September 30; in Petersburg the first two weeks of October; in Abingdon, Virginia, October 17-31; and in Bristol for several weeks after that. The Battle of Chickamauga took place September 19 and 20.

Chapter XIV:

1. Ben Rawlings reached home on November 26, the same day that the Federal army crossed the Rapidan and reached the Orange Turnpike and the Orange Plank Roads. With Meade thus in position to turn Lee's left and cut Confederate communications to Richmond, Lee moved east and occupied high ground south of Mine Run, a small tributary of the Rapidan. Meade found the

Confederates so strongly entrenched that he recrossed the Rapidan on December 1.

2. Brigadier General David Gregg's Second Division of Federal cavalry covered the Union left flank by reconnoitering southeast on the Brock Road and then west along the Catharpin Road toward Orange Courthouse. Rawlings' two prisoners were from Colonel J. Irvin Gregg's cavalry brigade, which had camped near White Hall the night of November 26-27. Most likely the men were from the Tenth New York Regiment, which marched in the advance on November 26, but as was customary, were in the rear the next morning.

3. Lieutenant Robert C. Shiver of the Second South Carolina Cavalry, part of Major General Pierce M. B. Young's brigade, commanded one of the Confederate patrols which skirmished with the advancing Federals on the Orange Plank Road on November 27.

4. Ben Rawlings was captured by either the Tenth New York, which moved north on the Orange Turnpike the morning of the 28th or by the Second Pennsylvania, which advanced to New Hope Church via White Hall and Parker's Store.

5. Mary Walker (1831-1919) was a graduate of Syracuse University and an assistant surgeon in the United States Army, the first woman to hold that position. After the Civil War, she fought for equal rights and woman suffrage. For a number of years, she wore a Bloomer costume of her own design but later dressed in masculine attire.

6. The Old Capitol Prison was a "temporary and hastily built substitute for the United States Capitol, burned by the British in 1812." The building was used later as a hotel and was in dilapidated condition when used as a prison during the Civil War.

7. Belle Boyd gained notoriety as a female spy for the Confederacy when she took information to Stonewall Jackson in Front Royal, Virginia, during his Valley Campaign of 1862. She

was confined at the Old Capitol during the summer of 1862 and again in 1863.

8.   Cleggett Fitzhugh, a Pennsylvania resident and Southern sympathizer, captured John E. Cook, one of John Brown's followers. Cook fled Harper's Ferry and was in hiding in Franklin County Pennsylvania, where Fitzhugh lived. Fitzhugh recognized and captured Cook when he left the woods in search of food. During the Antietam campaign, Fitzhugh joined Company K of the First Virginia Cavalry but was captured. He claimed to be a prisoner of war, but the Federal authorities treated him as a political prisoner who was "aiding and abetting the enemy, acting as a guide for the rebel General Longstreet."

9. Captain Julian P. Lee was a member of the Confederate Adjutant General's staff.

10.   Fort McHenry was used primarily as a distribution point for Confederate prisoners, who were then sent to such permanent locations as Point Lookout, Fort Delaware, and Johnson's Island. Rawlings was sent from Old Capitol to Fort McHenry on January 12, 1864, and from Fort McHenry to Point Lookout on January 23.

11.   Southern sympathizers in Baltimore sometimes smuggled food and money to the Confederate prisoners at Fort McHenry, and, in true capitalist tradition, those prisoners with money were permitted to buy vegetables from the sutlers. Health and wealth were closely connected at McHenry as well as at other prisons.

12.   Mrs. Lucy Woolfrey was the wife of Anderson Woolfrey, a cooper. They lived at the junction of the Orange Plank Road and the Germanna Ford Road (also called the Culpeper Plank Road). W. D. Foster was a farmer who lived near Ben Rawlings' home.

13.   John L. Rawlings was Ben Rawlings' cousin. In the 1860 census, John is listed as a mechanic. He was living with his

sister, Elizabeth, and her husband, Lewis A. Boggs, on the Boggs plantation. In 1862, he married Sarah Austin, governess for the Boggs' children.

14. Sadly, Lieutenant James T. Humphries, whose sash, pins, and military buttons Ben Rawlings had borrowed, died in September of 1864, probably of food poisoning, after eating food sent to him in a box from home.

Chapter XV:

1. Sibley tents, named for their designer, Henry H. Sibley, were lightweight cone-shaped tents, "erected on a tripod holding a single pole." As many as twelve men could be placed in one Sibley tent.

2. In the Spring of 1864, stories of the mistreatment of prisoners, both Union and Confederate, circulated in the North and South. William H. Hoffman, United States Commissary General of Prisoners, was convinced that the Confederacy was deliberately mistreating prisoners and ordered the rations in all Northern prisons reduced and the guard increased. Confederates believed in turn that their men in the Northern prisons were mistreated as well. The extent to which the directive for reduced rations in the Northern camps was enforced depended upon the individual prison commandant. A zealous Rebel-hater might return clothing sent to Confederate prisoners if it was not gray in color, while others, after an initial "crackdown," allowed the sutlers to operate and tolerated other amenities.

3. Fort Delaware was situated on low, marshy ground. The dampness and the sometimes salty drinking water contributed to the fort's unsavory reputation as a prison. With an adequate supply of money, however, even a Fort Delaware prisoner could improve considerably the conditions of his existence. Confederates who had Northern friends wrote to them and requested money, food, books and clothing. These requests were nearly always honored, although

131

one prisoner reported a refusal for aid, "*as I was a damn rebel and did not deserve any.*"

4. "The best government the world ever saw" and similar phrases were used to describe the United States government. Many Northern volunteers said they were fighting to preserve "the best government on earth."

5. In the fall of 1864, the political climate brought about a change in the Northern attitude toward prisoner exchange. Lincoln realized his re-election chances would improve if he heeded the public demand for prisoner exchange. Prisoners to be exchanged had to be well enough to travel but sick enough to be of no use to their respective armies for sixty days.

6. After Rawlings was exchanged, he was admitted to Hospital Number four in Richmond on October 17. His illness was "chronic diarrhea," an ailment which afflicted many Civil War soldiers as well as prisoners. He was furloughed November 11, 1864.

7. Rawlings' request for greenbacks and chewing tobacco reflected his need for some medium of financial exchange. Confederate prisoners whose families could not send greenbacks often sold or traded chewing tobacco to obtain food and clothing.

Chapter XVI:

1. The Howlett Line, south of James River and west of Bermuda Hundred, protected the vital Richmond and Petersburg Railroad. The Thirtieth Virginia was ordered to the extreme right of the Confederate lines at the end of March to oppose Sheridan's attempts to turn the Confederate right. The regiment was hotly engaged near Dinwiddie Court House on March 31. The next day Pickett withdrew toward Five Forks, a road junction so crucial to the Southside Railroad that Lee ordered Pickett to hold Five Forks "at all cost."

2. On April 1 at Five Forks, Corse's Brigade, on the right of the Confederate line, was nearly surrounded by the enemy after a gap developed between Pickett's left and the main Confederate line to the east. The brigade, along with the Ninth and Thirteenth Virginia Cavalry, and Pegram's artillery stood alone against overwhelming numbers of the Federal Fifth Corps and Sheridan's cavalry. "Corse's stalwarts" were always revered by Virginians as those who "stood fast to the end at Five Forks."

3. With his lines now broken, Lee had to abandon Richmond and Petersburg and retreat to the west along the railroad lines in an attempt to unite with Johnston's army in North Carolina. On April 6, the Thirtieth Virginia fought a last, desperate battle at Sayler's Creek when Pickett's men and a few other commands were cut off from the rest of the army. Corse was one of six generals captured that day.

4. The pursuing Federals blocked one railroad junction after another on the Richmond and Danville and the Southside Railroads. Surrender was Lee's only alternative when Sheridan captured the Confederate supplies at Appomattox Station, while Union cavalry and infantry blocked the road to Lynchburg on the morning of April 9, 1865.

5. On the day that Lee surrendered at Appomattox, Benjamin Rawlings was "twenty years and three months old." He went to Richmond and received his official parole on May 2, 1865.

Chapter XVII:

1. This letter was published in the *Virginia Magazine of History and Biography*, LXXV (1967): 459-65. It is used by permission of the Virginia Historical Society.

Selected Bibliography

Manuscripts

Chapel Hill, North Carolina. University of North Carolina Library. Southern Historical Collection.

> Haskell, Alexander Cheeves. Letters, January-May, 1861.
> McMichael, Paul Agalus. Civil War Diary, 1864-1865.
> Spain, Harwell Percy. Diary of activities in Charleston, January 3 to March 17, 1861.
> Woodley, Andrew. Narrative of war service at Fort Sumter, 1861.

Durham, North Carolina. Perkins Library, Duke University.

> Wise, George. Civil War Diary.

Fredericksburg, Virginia. Fredericksburg-Spotsylvania National Military Park. Thirtieth Virginia Infantry Regiment Papers.

> Hirsh, Isaac. Diary, 2 vols.
> Kidd, W. B. Diary.
> Mansfield, Roger. Notes from tombstones and church records in Spotsylvania County.
> Stuart, Meriwether. Outline of activities of Thirtieth Virginia Infantry Regiment.
> _____. Roster of Thirtieth Virginia Infantry Regiment.
> Young, Marquis Lafayette. Letters
> Young, T. S., and Young, Ot. Letters.

Richmond, Virginia. Virginia State Library.

> Knox-Gordon Family Genealogical Notes.

Richmond, Virginia. Virginia Historical Society.

> Journal of Lizzie Maxwell Alsop, 1862.

Letter of Hannah Garlick Rawlings, 1865. Published in *Virginia Magazine of History and Biography*, LXXV (1967): 459-65.

Roswell, Georgia. Private collection of Florence Swift Durrance.

Rawlings Family Papers.

Books

Benedict, George Grenville. *Vermont in the Civil War: A History of the Part Taken by the Vermont Soldiers and Sailors in the War for the Union, 1861-5.* 2 vols. Burlington, Vermont, 1888.

Black, Robert C. *The Railroads of the Confederacy.* Chapel Hill, 1952.

Boatner, Mark Mayo III. *The Civil War Dictionary.* New York, 1959.

Bradley, Philip, comp. *An Index to the Waverly Novels.* Metuchen, N.J., 1975.

Bruce, Kathleen. *Virginia Iron Manufacture in the Slave Era.* New York and London, 1930.

Byrd, William, "A Progress to the Mines," in the *Prose Works of William Byrd of Westover.* Edited by Louis B. Wright. Cambridge, Mass., 1966.

Caldwell, J. F. J. *The History of a Brigade of South Carolinians Known First as "Gregg's" and Subsequently as "McGowan's" Brigade.* Philadelphia, 1866.

Campbell, Joseph. *The Hero with a Thousand Faces.* New York, 1949.

Cash, Wilbur J. *The Mind of the South.* New York, 1941.

Catton, Bruce. *The Centennial History of the Civil War.* 3 vols. Garden City, N.Y., 1961.

Chambers, Lenior. *Stonewall Jackson.* New York, 1959.

Chesnut, Mary Boykin. *A Diary from Dixie* or *Mary Chesnut's Civil War.* Edited by C. Vann Woodward. New Haven and London, 1981.

Clark, James H. *The Iron-Hearted Regiment: Being an Account of the*

Battles, Marches, and Gallant Deeds Performed by the 115 Regiment N.Y. Volunteers. Albany, N.Y., 1865.

Cooke, John Esten. *Mohun: or, The Last Days of Lee and His Paladins*. New York, 1869.

———. *Surry of Eagle's Nest*. New York, 1894; first published in 1866.

Craven, Avery Odelle. *Edmund Ruffin, Southerner: A Study in Secession*. New York, 1932.

Dictionary of American Biography. 120 vols. Edited by Allen Johnson and Dumas Malone. New York, 1928-1944.

Eaton, Clement. *The Growth of Southern Civilization, 1790-1860*. New York, 1963; first published in 1961.

Erikson, Erik H. *Identity and the Life Cycle*. New York, 1959.

Evans, Clement A., gen. ed. *Confederate Military History*. 12 vols. Atlanta, 1899.

Fishwick, Marshall William. *American Heroes: Myth and Reality*. Washington, 1954.

———. *Lee After the War*. New York, 1963.

Freeman, Douglas Southall. *Lee's Lieutenants: A Study in Command*. 3 vols. New York, 1942-1944.

Freidel, Frank B., ed. *Harvard Guide to American History*. 2 vols. Cambridge, Mass., 1974.

Harwell, Richard B. *Songs of the Confederacy*. New York, 1959.

Hesseltine, William B. *Civil War Prisons*. New York, 1930.

Hinton, Richard J. *John Brown and His Men*. New York, 1894.

Johnson, John Lipscomb. *Autobiographical Notes*. Privately printed, 1958.

Johnson, Robert Underwood, and Buel, C. C., eds. *Battles and Leaders of the Civil War*. 3 vols. New York, 1883-1887.

Kane, Harnett. *Spies for the Blue and Gray*. Garden City, N.Y., 1954.

Keegan, John. *The Face of Battle*. New York, 1976.

Krick, Robert K. *30th Virginia Infantry*. Lynchburg, Va., 1983.

Lefler, Hugh Talmage, and Newsome, Albert Ray. *North Carolina: The History of a Southern State*. rev. ed. Chapel Hill, 1963; first published in 1954.

Long, E. B., with Long, Barbara. *The Civil War Day by Day: An Almanac 1861-1865*. Garden City, N.Y., 1971.

Lord, Walter, ed. *The Fremantle Diary*. Boston, 1954; first published in England in 1863; rpt. New York and Mobile, 1864.

Mansfield, James Roger. *A History of Early Spotsylvania*. Orange, Virginia, 1977.

Massey, Mary Elizabeth. *Refugee Life in the Confederacy*. Baton Rouge, 1964.

Matthews, Mitford, ed. *Dictionary of Americanisms*. Chicago, 1951.

Merrill, Samuel Hill. *The Campaigns of the First Maine and First D. of C. Cavalry*. Portland, Maine, 1866.

Moore, John Hammond. *Research Material in South Carolina*. Columbia, S.C., 1967.

Morton, Richard. *Colonial Virginia*. 2 vols. Chapel Hill, 1960.

Murfin, James V. *The Gleam of Bayonets*. New York, 1965.

Olmstead, Frederick Law. *The Cotton Kingdom*. Edited by A. M. Schlesinger. New York, 1952; first published in 1861.

The Oxford English Dictionary, Oxford, England, 1933.

Randall, J. G., and Donald, David H. *The Civil War and Reconstruction*. 2nd rev. ed. Lexington, Mass., 1969.

Rust, Richard Dilworth, ed. *Glory and Pathos: Responses of Nineteenth Century American Authors to the Civil War*. Boston, 1970.

Shaara, Michael. *The Killer Angels*. New York, 1974.

Swem, Earl Gregg. *Virginia Historical Index*. 2 vols. 1934; rpt. Gloucester, Mass., 1965.

Taylor, William R. *Cavalier and Yankee*. New York, 1961.

Torrence, Clayton, comp. *Virginia Wills and Administrations 1632-1800*. Baltimore, 1965.

Twain, Mark. *Life on the Mississippi*. New York, 1906.

Sayre, Robert F. *The Examined Self: Benjamin Franklin, Henry Adams, Henry James*. Princeton, N.J., 1964.

United States Department of War. *Atlas to Accompany the Official Records of the Union and Confederate Armies*. Washington, D.C., 1891-1895.

United States Department of War. *War of the Rebellion: A Compilation of the Official Records of Union and Confederate Armies*. 70 vols. Edited by Robert N. Scott, et al. Washington, D.C., 1880-1901.

Wiley, Bell Irvin. *The Life of Billy Yank*. Indianapolis and New York, 1952.

_____. *The Life of Johnny Reb: The Common Soldier of the Confederacy*. Garden City, N.Y., 1971; first published in 1943.

Williams, Harry T. "The Military Leadership of North and South," in *Why the North Won the Civil War*. Edited by David Donald. Baton Rouge, 1960. Rpt. in *American Defense Policy and Perspective: From Colonial Times to the Present*. Edited by Raymond G. O'Connor. New York, 1965.

Wilson, Edmund. *Patriotic Gore*. New York, 1962.

Writers Program of W. P. A. in Virginia. *Virginia: Guide to the Old Dominion*. New York, 1941.

Articles

Abbott, Martin. "The First Shot at Fort Sumter." *Civil War History* III (March 1957): 41-45.

Auden, W. H. "The Quest Hero." *Texas Quarterly* IV (Winter 1961): 81-93.

Boyle, Francis Atherton. "The Prison Diary of Adjutant Francis Atherton Boyle, C.S.A." Edited by Mary Lindsay Thornton. *North Carolina Historical Review* XXXIX (December 1962): 58-84.

Catton, Bruce. "Prison Camps of the Civil War." *American Heritage* X (August 1959): 4-8; 96-97.

Cox, James. "Autobiography and America." *Virginia Quarterly Review* XLVII (Spring 1971): 252-277.

Goolrick, Frances Bernard. "Suffering in Fredericksburg." *Southern Historical Society Papers* XXXVII (1909): 355-359.

Hesseltine, William B. "Civil War Prisons -- Introduction." *Civil War History* VIII (June 1962): 117-120.

Howarth, William L. "Some Principles of Autobiography." *New Literary History* V (1974): 363-381.

Jones, J. William, comp. "The Treatment of Prisoners During the War Between the States." *Southern Historical Society Papers* I (1876): 113-227.

Krick, Robert K. "Maxcy Gregg: Political Extremist and Confederate General." *Civil War History* XIX (April 1973): 3-23.

Parker, F. L. "The Battle of Fort Sumter as Seen from Morris
    Island." *South Carolina Historical Magazine* (April 1969):
    65-71.
Ruffin, Edmund. Extracts from the unpublished Diary of Edmund
Ruffin, "The First Shot at Fort Sumter." *William and Mary
    Quarterly*, 1st ser., XX (October 1911): 69-101.
Spengemen, William C., and Lundquist, L. R. "Autobiography and
    the American Myth." *American Quarterly* XVII (Fall 1965):
    501-519.
Theodore, Terry. "The Confederate Theater." Pt. 1. *The Lincoln
    Herald* LXXVI (Winter 1974): 187-195; Pt. 2. *The Lincoln
    Herald* LXXVII (Spring 1974): 33-41.
Witherspoon, T. D. "Prison Life at Fort McHenry." *Southern
    Historical Society Papers* VIII (1880): 77-82; 111-119; 163-
    168.

Microfilm

Genealogical Society Film of the Church of Jesus Christ of the
Latter Day Saints.

Daughters of the American Revolution. Virginia
Genealogical Records, 1700-1900, Rockbridge County,
Virginia. Film 0850094.
Deed Books C-D, 1734-1751, Spotsylvania County,
Virginia. Film 0034069.
Deed Books KK-LL, 1842-1846, Spotsylvania County,
Virginia. Film 0034084.
Deed Books MM-NN, 1846-1852, Spotsylvania County,
Virginia. Film 0034084.
Deed Books OO-PP, 1852-1857, Spotsylvania County,
Virginia. Film 0034085.
Deed Books SS, 1865-1869, Spotsylvania County, Virginia.
Film 0034041.
General Index to Wills, 1722-1947, Books A-B, 1722-1759,
Spotsylvania, County, Virginia. Film 0034055.
Index to Deeds, Grantors, 1733-1922, Spotsylvania County,
Virginia. Film 0034066.

Wills, Inventories, and Account Books, Indexed, XI-XII, 1848-1884, Orange County, Virginia. Film 0033008.
1860 U.S. Slave Schedules -- Virginia. Film 0905397.

Ruffin, Edmund. Diary. 14 vols. 1856-1865. Washington, D.C.: Library of Congress microfilm. Shelf no. 13, 743, reel 2, vol. 3, Aug. 5, 1859-July 31, 1860: vol. 4, Aug., 1860-May, 1861.
South Carolina Compiled Service Records, First South Carolina Volunteers (Six Months, 1861). Washington, D.C.: National Archives Microfilm, Microcopy 267, roll 146.
United States Department of Commerce. *Seventh Census of the United States*. Washington, D.C.: National Archives. Spotsylvania County, Virginia, microcopy T-6, roll 941.
_____. *Eighth Census of the United States*. Washington, D.C.: National Archives. Orange County, Virginia, microcopy T-7, roll 301; Spotsylvania County, Virginia, microcopy T-7, roll 299; Spotsylvania County, Virginia Slave Schedules, microcopy 653, roll 1397.
_____. *Ninth Census of the United States*. Washington, D.C.: National Archives. Rockbridge County, Virginia, microcopy T-8, roll 1640; Spotsylvania County, Virginia, microcopy T-8, roll 1641.
Virginia Compiled Service Records, Thirtieth Virginia Infantry Regiment. Washington, D.C.: National Archives Microfilm, microcopy T-8, roll 1640.

Newspapers on Microfilm

Charleston *Daily Courier*, January-May, 1861.
Fredericksburg *Christian Banner*, 1862, I, no. 2, 5, 7, 8, 11; May 17, 20; June 7, 14, 18; July 2.
Fredericksburg *News*, 1848-1860.
Fredericksburg *Virginia Herald*, March 11, 1862.
Fredericksburg *Weekly Advertiser*, January 10, 1857-December 22, 1860.
Richmond *Daily Dispatch*, April-May, 1861.
Richmond *Enquirer*, September 2, 1864.

Richmond *Examiner*, September 4, 1863.
Valley *Virginian*, 1868-1876.
Wilmington *Daily Journal*, April 23, 26, 1861.

Letters, Interviews, and Clippings

Durrance, Florence Swift. Gainesville, Florida. Interview. January 26, 1977.

King, George H. S., to Byrd B. Tribble, November 29, 1976; March 1, 1977.

"Professor R. H. Rawlings Tells of His Interesting Career," newspaper clipping, no name or date, in author's possession.

Rawlings, Florence Baker. Fredericksburg, Virginia. Interview. August 18, 1976.

Stuart, Meriwether, to Byrd B. Tribble. April 30, 1976.

Stuart, Meriwether, to Lillian Rawlings Swift. January 24, 1959.

INDEX

First South Carolina Volunteers *see South Carolina Troops*
    also see Richland Rifles
Fitzhugh, Cleggett 77, 130
Five Forks, Battle of i, 95, 104, 132-133
Florida 15, 99, 114
Florida Military Academy 118
Florence, SC 2-3, 7
Food and clothing 1, 3, 35, 52, 64, 68-69, 72, 78, 82-87, 89, 91, 93-
    95, 97-98, 107-108, 130-131
Foote, Shelby 125
"Forest Hill" 118
Foster, Capt. Henry L. 55, 59
Foster, W. D. 79, 89-90, 130
"Found your mule" 36, 119
Franklin County, PA 130
Franklin, Gen. William F. 123
Frayser's Farm, Battle of [White Oak Swamp] 102, 122
Frazier, Herndon 26, 117
Frazier, Martha Rawlings [aunt] 117
Fredericksburg, Battle of 64-65, 102-103
Fredericksburg, VA 1, 7, 26, 28-29, 31, 35-37, 41, 61-64, 72, 102-
    103, 118, 120, 126-127
Fredericksburg *News* Newspaper 7, 28, 113
Fredericksburg *Free Lance* Newspaper 106-107
Fredericksburg *Star* Newspaper 109
French's Battery 50
French, Capt. 45, 50
French leave 31, 118
Ft. Delaware 86, 93-94, 103, 130-131
Ft. Donelson 38
Ft. Fisher 102
Ft. Harrison 95
Ft. Johnson 115
Ft. McHenry 78, 84, 130
Ft. Monroe 87
Ft. Moultrie 16, 116
Ft. Pinckney 16
Ft. Sumter i, ii, 7, 14, 16-17, 25-26, 28, 30, 85, 103-104, 110, 113-
    117

Front Royal, VA 129
Funkhouser, M. S. 104
Furlough and Bounty Act 120
Gaines Mill, Battle of 43, 102, 121
Gaines, William E. 102-103
Germanna Ford Road [Culpeper Plank Road] 130
Gettysburg Campaign 70, 102, 128
Gibbs, Florence Virginia [wife of Benjamin Rawlings] 100-101, 110
Gibbs, James E. A. 100-101, 110
Gibbs, Surgeon General 4
Gibbes, W. Hampton 7
Goldsboro, NC 1, 4, 38, 113, 120
Goochland County, VA 93, 96
Gordon, Sgt. 107
Gouldin, Major John Milton 35, 69
Grant, Gen. U. S. 96
"Green Hill" 117
Greenville, VA 108
Gregg, Gen. David 129
Gregg, Maxcy 8, 11-12, 17, 20, 22, 25, 28-30, 64, 103, 106, 110, 114, 117
Grove Hill, AL 9, 20, 22
Guiney's Station 65
Guy Mannering iii-iv
Hadensville, VA 93, 96
Hagerstown Pike 124
Haislip, Joe 59
Hall, Col. E. D. 125
Hamilton, A. H. 101
Hamilton's Crossing 64
Hammond Hospital 89-90
Hampton, Wade 6, 114
Hanover Court House, VA 70
Hardee's Tactics 33
Hardtack 35
Harper's Ferry 45, 49-50, 52, 54-55, 103, 123-124, 130
Harris 40-41, 121
Harris, Clem 72

Powell, James 90
Preston, John 4, 6-8, 11, 15, 114
Purcell's Battery 35
Railroad battery 16
Raphine, VA i, 100-101, 103-104, 108, 110-111
Rapidan River 123, 128
Rapidan Station 123
Rappahannock River 31, 64, 72, 118, 126-127
Rawlings, Ann Cason [mother] 82, 90-91, 93
Rawlings, Benjamin [uncle] 9, 20, 26
Rawlings, Benjamin Cason family history   ii, iii, v; leaves home, travels to Charleston i, 1-4, 7, 30, 103, 106, 110; meets John Preston 4, 7; enlists in SC regiment i, 11, 20, 30, 41, 103, 106, 110; first Virginia volunteer for the South ii, 103, 111; life of early recruits 11; challenged to duel ii, 11, 14; newspapers extol his actions as early volunteer i, 7-8, 28-29; volunteers as sharpshooter 14, 16; witnesses surrender of Ft. Sumter ii, 17, 103, 110; Virginia secedes 25; SC troops reluctant to go to Virginia 25, 117; SC troops feted on trip to Richmond i, 25-27; returns home as hero   ii, 6; offered post of Orderly Sergeant in 30th VA Regiment   26, 103; receives discharge from SC regiment 28-30, 103, 106, 110; joins Mt. Pleasant Rifles of 30th VA 28, 31, 103, 106, 110-111; arrested for taking "French" leave 31; demonstrates coolness under fire 33; has measles, unable to go to Manassas 35; winter quarters (1861-62) 36-37; re-enlists 38, 120; elected first lieutenant ii, 38, 103, 111; Peninsula Campaign   43-44, 120-122; march to Loudoun Heights 45, 122-125; takes Co. D to top of Loudoun Heights   50; explores Harper's Ferry   52-54; returns to regiment with plunder   54; fights near Dunkard Church and Mumma Farm i, 55-57, 107, 124-125; describes battlefield ii, 57, 59; Shepherdstown hospitality 61; Battle of Fredericksburg 64-65, 126-127; Fredericksburg refugees 64, 126; paper collar ridiculed 65, 127; snowball battle 66-67, 127; siege of Suffolk 68-69; promoted to captain   ii, 68, 111; regiment not at Gettysburg   70, 128; in Southwestern Virginia and Eastern Tennessee 70-72, 128; capture and imprisonment *see Capture and Imprisonment*; returns to regiment i, 95, 103, 104, 111, 132; retreat to Appomattox i, 96, 104, 111, 132-133; attempts

151